ARTISTS IN WIGAN SCHOOLS:

A RIGHT FOR ALL CHILDREN

by Rod Taylor

Published by the Calouste Gulbenkian Foundation, London, 1991.

Dedication

This book is dedicated to the memory of Dave Burton who felt he'd found in Drumcroon and the Artists in Wigan Schools Scheme an embodiment of his own educational vision. Had he been granted the time he would have striven to bring about something similar in his area of Yorkshire.

Contents

Foreword

The Gulbenkian Foundation's involvement with the developments described here began in 1985 when we received a grant application from the Wigan Education Authority to enable local artists to work in selected primary schools. Although such applications were not uncommon, the Wigan proposal contained a number of unusual features. To begin with, the application came from an education authority and not, as might have been expected, from an arts organisation or from individual artists. Also, the artists in question were not well-established, which is normally the case with visiting artists, but had recently graduated from local Art Colleges.

Artists in Wigan Schools is essentially their story, but the involvement of the Local Authority, and of Rod Taylor its Art Adviser, in particular, is a vital part of that story. None of the pioneering developments described in this book would have taken place had he and his colleagues not held the view that the visual arts should permeate children's education and that they are entitled, not simply to an acceptable level of provision, but to the very best that the Authority, local schools and visiting artists can collectively deliver.

By asking Rod Taylor to write this book we hope that the example of Wigan's commitment to the arts in schools will reach beyond those many people who are already familiar with it. The book appears, we realise, at a time when the secure local authority structure that gave rise to these initiatives is dissolving, and more responsibility is being handed over to schools. To what extent these circumstances will inhibit the kind of initiatives recounted here remains to be seen. Meanwhile, if schools of the future require proof of the extraordinary riches that artists and children can create between them, this book provides it.

Simon Richey
Assistant Director, Education
Calouste Gulbenkian Foundation, UK Branch

Author's Note

One of the themes running through *Artists in Wigan Schools* is that of partnership and co-operation in the best interests of young people. So, not surprisingly, many people have made contributions to this book. Especially significant is that provided by Wigan's Director of Education, J K Hampson, without whose unswerving support the book could never have been written. Equally important is his conviction that it is necessary to provide the right people with the right space in order to foster their creativity: this has been central to the innovative achievements which have taken place in arts education in Wigan, and which have a direct bearing on the content of this book.

Special thanks are due to all my friends and colleagues at the Drumcroon Education Art Centre which serves as the headquarters of the Wigan Art and Design Service. The Service includes advisory support, the educational work at the Turnpike Gallery, the administration of the Wigan Schools Loan Collection and the Artists in Wigan Schools Scheme. But for the professionalism of these friends and colleagues I would have found it impossible to focus on the considerable demands of writing this book. In addition, their ideas and practice have been crucial to the ever-evolving ways in which Wigan has harnessed the special skills of artists. Likewise, their commitment to monitoring and documenting a range of residencies ensured that there was an abundance of material available to draw upon. Particular mention must be made of Bryan Edmondson who, since 1987, has taken responsibility for the day-by-day running and organisation of the Artists in Wigan Schools Scheme.

Thanks are also due to all the artists who have worked in the Scheme, whether salaried or on an Enterprise basis, and on shorter-term Drumcroon and Turnpike Gallery residencies. The work of some artists and the details of some residencies have had to be omitted because of the pressures on space. However, many do feature, some in-depth, some in passing, and they provide the core of the text. I am particularly grateful to those who provided detailed information and insights through recorded interviews.

Artists in Wigan Schools also draws upon the testimonies of many Wigan head teachers and classroom teachers. These have been provided through interviews and written statements, much of it in relation to Drumcroon and Turnpike exhibitions and other events involving artists and their pupils. As virtually all Wigan schools have had experience of working with artists, they too have provided a wealth of material. Another important dimension has been added through the testimonies of the numerous art educators from all over the country and from abroad who have come to Wigan to see what has been taking place. I am grateful to them for their letters and reports: their viewpoints have provided invaluable information.

It has also been a pleasure to work in close co-operation with the Calouste Gulbenkian Foundation. Their Assistant Director (Education), Simon Richey, has shown a warm interest and faith in the Artists in Wigan Schools Scheme since its earliest days. His advice, promptings and suggestions have always been eminently sensible and practical, and his quiet support has been an important motivation during a period when the demands of a busy work schedule could so easily have proved a total disruption to the writing of this book.

Finally, special thanks to Kathleen Mather and Irene Wilcock for the patience and thoroughness they have shown in typing their respective sections of the manuscript; where there have been errors, they have invariably been mine, not theirs!

Introduction

It has been my privilege to work in Wigan since it became a metropolitan authority in 1974. As the Authority's Art Adviser I was involved in setting up the Drumcroon Education Art Centre and am its Director. The Centre opened in late 1980 and rapidly became the focal point for an ambitious local authority seeking to reach and 'touch' all Wigan's young people. Another important development was the creation of the Artists in Wigan Schools Scheme in 1984. The Centre and the Scheme have become central planks of the Authority's education service.

For most of my time in Wigan the raising of educational standards has been high on the national agenda and the Authority has achieved national recognition for the quality of the support and services to schools across the curriculum. Success measured in external examination terms is matched by the vitality, richness and excitement of what is on offer. When unemployment levels and socio-economic factors are taken into account, not only is the record outstanding but the relevance of the service becomes fully apparent.

Wigan is in Greater Manchester, more or less in the centre of a triangle formed by the cities of Liverpool, Manchester and Preston. Its 320,000 population makes it one of the largest metropolitan authorities. Coal mining was the main industry: its decline was a major contributor to unemployment, rising well above 20% when recession was at its most severe in the early 1980s. There has been much deprivation in the area which, nevertheless, retains a buoyancy; and attitudes and outlook remain positive.

This is particularly so with regard to the education approaches adopted since 1974. The Entitlement Curriculum Policy was designed to address the needs of all young people. This has proved invaluable in helping schools to formulate whole school policies, ensuring coherence and continuity in pupils' education and, more recently, for dealing with the demands and requirements of the National Curriculum. Central to Wigan thinking and to the Entitlement Curriculum Policy are the Seven Wigan Principles (1). They state that

1. Education must look forward and recognise that it is the means of preparing people for a future of which we have little or no conception.

2. Education must take place within an international context as opposed to the national context within which it has operated to date.

3. Education must respond equally to the needs of all individuals. The needs of individual people may be different but any one need is of no greater importance than any other.

4. Education must free the individual to enable the expression of human uniqueness.

5. Education must take cognisance of the rights of the individual and encourage mutual respect between individuals and between ethnic and cultural groups.

6. Education should equip people with the desire and skills to participate in a democratic society.

7. Education must encourage awareness of the fact that society exists only as a combination of the many and varied roles of individuals within a structured framework.

These Principles include a broad view of a curriculum constructed around certain areas of experience: the Social and Cultural, the Technological, the Aesthetic, the Physical, the Communicative, the Spiritual, Economic and Political, Mathematical, and Scientific. Through active involvement in such initiatives as the national Arts in Schools Project, considerable numbers of teachers have been able to step back, come to terms with these broad issues and effectively reappraise their classroom practice.

Wigan's success by the commonly applied criteria - such as examination results - has been achieved with the arts being seen as central to learning. In recent years Wigan has developed an unusually high arts profile. Its central resources have operated with the needs of all young people in mind, rather than catering for the privileged few. Pitprop Theatre, Ludus Dance and centres for Drama, Music and Media Education contribute to a unique service in which the visual arts have played a particularly influential and pioneering role. These services flourish at the subject-specific level and contribute richly to the wider curriculum, as emphasised in the Wigan Arts Policy Statement. It demonstrates how they contribute to each of the areas of experience, to personal and social education and race, gender and special education needs etc as well as to teaching styles, pupil roles, negotiated learning and the recording of achievement.

Within a year of Drumcroon opening it had become the host to the influential national Critical Studies in Art Education (CSAE) Project, of which I was Director from 1981-84, and which was funded by the Arts, Crafts and Schools Councils. Through this Project, Drumcroon became known to many art educators. The Project arose out of a concern that the majority of young people in England and Wales were leaving school with experience of making art but with little or no knowledge, understanding or sense of enjoyment of the wider world of the visual arts practised by others. The book to which it gave rise, *Educating for Art*, (Longman, 1986), clarifies the principles upon which the Wigan Art and Design Service is founded. These are consistent with the Wigan Principles and provide criteria whereby those in the Service join with teachers in an attempt to reach and benefit all the young people being educated in Wigan.

Drumcroon is closely connected with the Turnpike Gallery, with which it is now 'twinned', providing two gallery venues for visiting groups of pupils. Through the Wigan Schools Loan Service, all schools can have access to original works of art, while the Artists in Wigan Schools Scheme provides the fourth element in the Authority's Art and Design Service on offer to all schools.

Crucial to the development of this Scheme was the support given by the Calouste Gulbenkian Foundation, with whom there was always an unwritten agreement that eventually I would document the history and significance of the Scheme with the intention of stimulating initiatives elsewhere. It is being written at a time when others are similarly engaged in writing about artists-in-residence; *Artists in Schools: a Handbook for Teachers and Artists* by Caroline Sharp and Karen Dust (Bedford Square Press, 1990) was the first of these to be published. All are likely to place emphasis on the educational criteria for residencies. These are in contrast to some of the writing generated by the early residencies, which were criticised for allegedly serving the interests of artists in an age when Church and Medici had ceased to support them - children should not be used as guinea pigs, went the argument.

These concerns were clearly expressed in two books published in 1978; *Artists and People* by Su Braden published in this country and *Artists-in-Schools: Analysis and Criticism*, edited by Ralph Smith, in the United States. Su Braden documents one residency in which the artist

"...found the structure of the school quite difficult to comprehend and, being naturally insular, spent the first few months in his studio, meeting very few people and not even eating in the canteen. It seems that no one approached him either."

After a number of forays into the school and some attempts to communicate

"... he withdrew to the private studio where he spent the last few months of his residency in his former state of isolation absorbed in his 'own' work." (2)

The wrong artist in the wrong place leads to a sad experience for all concerned. Further cynicism about school residencies was expressed by Ralph Smith, who argued that "asking artists to educate school and community merely complicates and interferes with their work", therefore "let artists do what they do best where they do it best". In the same book Kenneth Morantz amplifies these sentiments in caricature form in 'A Parable'.

"And they took lion from his home and placed him in a zoo. And they provided for his needs with space to roam and plenty to eat. But, said his keepers, you must not go beyond these limits, nor may you hunt your food. And every day from 9.00 in the morning until 5.00 in the evening and sometimes at night people will come to look at you; and they expect you to roar and claw the bark from trees and tear at the hunks of meat we throw to you so they might learn what a lion does.
And thus did man in his infinite wisdom, create a Lion-in-Residence." (3)

Humorous - but what a strangely nineteenth century view of the starving artist in a garret, divorced from society. The pioneering young artists of the Wigan Scheme previously had to make do with bedroom or garden shed as studios - certainly not the best places in which to "do it best". They constantly say that they need and enjoy contact with others - that it is actually beneficial to their art.

In the United States book, Eliot Eisner suggests that "Artists are presumably able to do what Art teachers are not competent to do." For all I know, teachers' jobs may have been put in jeopardy by the introduction of artists into United States schools, but throughout *Artists and Schools: Analysis and Criticism* there is certainly no reference to artist and teacher working together. By contrast, the Artists in Wigan Schools Scheme has been founded upon the principle of partnership. It is our belief that when teacher and artist come together, each recognising that the other has special skills, young people benefit to a greater degree than can be achieved when each - however brilliant - is operating in isolation.

The Wigan Art and Design Service operates from Drumcroon, so this is the natural base for the artists. They are the main agency through which Drumcroon principles are taken outwards into the schools. The Drumcroon Policy Statement, consistent with the Wigan Principles, is therefore also relevant to the artists within the Scheme. It aims

"To give all Wigan's young people - irrespective of age - their teachers and the local community access to the range, breadth and variety of the visual arts through the main focus of contemporary makers, taking into account such issues as race, gender and special needs. To give further insight and understanding, the Centre provides its visitors with opportunities to engage in practical activities and it attempts to place each exhibition into a contextual framework by demonstrating process through resident artists and craftspeople and through the use of secondary source material which has the potential to range across time, place and cultures."

By 1984 Drumcroon had considerable experience of utilising the skills of artists; the Artists in Wigan Schools Scheme can therefore be seen as having grown out of Drumcroon. By virtue of its central role Drumcroon naturally commands the opening chapter of this book.

1

Drumcroon

"The Drumcroon Education Art Centre... encourages and complements the work of local primary and secondary schools and, by means of an enterprising series of workshops, exhibitions and artists-in-schools schemes, it brings children into fruitful contact with professional artists and students in further and higher education."

Anthony Dyson 'Art and Design: A Parting of Ways', *Curriculum Progress 5-16: School Subjects and the National Curriculum Debate*, 1989 (1)

Having opened in November 1980, Drumcroon during its short life has had "a profound influence on the development of Art, Craft and Design education in Britain", according to Anthony Dyson. The Centre is housed close to Wigan town centre in a converted, castellated 1903 doctor's house and surgery with care taken to retain its intimate, domestic character. An important concern at Drumcroon is that visitors should encounter art in a warm environment, one that young people in particular can relate to.

"This philosophy underpinned a cunning and creative use of space, in large part responsible for the Centre's success with pupils and the general public, many of whom have been introduced through visits to Drumcroon to a world of art and design that would otherwise pass them by." (2)

In order to create large enough gallery spaces in the Centre, rounded archways were added to join lounge and dining room areas; two rooms were opened up on the first floor to create a conference room for teachers' meetings and talks to the general public; and two smaller rooms were linked to relate an artist's studio to exhibition space. A coffee lounge, library area, photographic dark room, schools loan area and a further artist's studio hint at the wide range of activities and resources housed within the building.

Much of the Centre's activities are planned around six exhibitions each year spanning half-termly periods, with one designed to cover the summer holiday when the Centre remains open for more informal use. Occasional use is made of touring exhibitions, but most are conceived and organised by the Centre staff with their educational usage fully considered. In constructing the exhibition programme, certain criteria are kept in mind: What balance should there be between exhibitions with immediate appeal and those which are thought-provoking? How might the in-depth exploration of single artists' works relate over a period of time to group shows exploring particular themes or processes, etc? To what extent does a particular year's programme adequately embrace the breadth of art and design activities and issues currently being explored and practised? Are technological concerns being represented? Is there a correct balance in race and gender terms? The crite-

The Main Gallery seen from the entrance. The catalogue and visitors' book stand made by Denise Bellamy - an artist in the Wigan School Scheme.

Christine Kowal Post in residence during the 1988 British Relief Woodcarving exhibition, discussing the work and methods of an African sculptor friend.

A young visitor, lost in contemplation, caresses the red car in a Kowal Post carving while looking up at the works of Elzbieta Lepa.

ria are so complex that the staff now look at the balance over a much longer time than one year.

Each school year's programme is advertised during the previous year, enabling schools to book sufficiently in advance and to integrate visits into classroom practice: well over 50 schools, for example, had booked for the June 1989 'Fragments' exhibition by the previous November. Each school receives teachers' notes, a poster, catalogue and invitations to each preview. A meeting to which the exhibiting artist normally contributes further ensures that teachers are as fully informed as possible, and much informal discussion takes place over a long period of time.

Once within the Centre visiting groups find themselves in a stimulating, sometimes profuse, yet carefully ordered environment. Displayed works are contextualised through the use of preliminary studies, sketches, location shots and other related material; and complemented by reproductions and book material drawn from the well-stocked library reference section. This material is selected by the Centre staff and poses questions about the content, form, process and mood of the exhibited works. What are they about and how have they been ordered and arranged? How have they been executed and with what? What moods, atmospheres or feelings do they convey or encapsulate? Which other artists across time, place and cultures, have addressed similar themes, issues and concerns? Which examples most effectively establish links with the works on display? This model (content, form, process, mood) helps to ensure that interviews with artists address all aspects of their work and helps the compilation of catalogues; teachers' notes are likewise constructed around the model, thus linking with the catalogue statements. Numerous schools now make systematic use of this content, form, process, mood model, providing their pupils with a powerful analytical tool to help their engagements with art works, and to enable them to relate classroom and gallery practice.

There is no single prescribed method of usage: negotiation between Centre and school is encouraged to ensure maximum engagement with what is on offer and the integration of gallery experience with classroom practice. However, many primary schools choose to spend full days in the Centre, dividing their time between the exhibited works and related workshop activities. Gallery discussions frequently involve them for a whole morning, some formal, some informal. Practical workshop time is inevitably limited, but this does not really matter because what they undertake

a) is more to do with process than product. It is through reference to possible related activities con-

tained within the teachers' notes and the teacher's involvement in the day that longer-term follow-up work can take place in the classroom.

b) is related in some way to exhibition content. Use of the content, form, process, mood model once again ensures that activities can reflect the full scope of the exhibited works and their potential, or that the chosen way in is knowingly selected.

c) is based on first-hand experience, demanding that pupils respond to the world around and within them as well as to qualities within the exhibited works, though the latter will inevitably inform the former.

Young people from nursery age through to sixth form and tertiary levels use the Centre, so do higher education groups from all over the country, some visiting annually.

Authority-wide initiatives

The Turnpike Gallery, seven miles away in Leigh town centre, offers a complementary exhibition programme built around the same principles: in any given year countless young people are afforded opportunities to engage with original works in a properly structured gallery context. This is reflected in the writing of *The Sunday Times* art critic Marina Vaizey who visited Wigan in May 1987 when the Drumcroon 'Joie de Vivre' exhibition provided the focus for an authority-wide 'Print Extravaganza'. In relating the Drumcroon exhibition to these other activities, Vaizey provided an account of how the Entitlement needs of vast numbers of young people were being addressed.

"The current level of activity is, in a word, stupendous...Over half-terms, 3,000 schoolchildren visit both Drumcroon and the Turnpike...exhibitions are in turn integrated with exhibitions in the schools from the big loan collection owned by Wigan..." (3)

With over 1,000 works being in schools at any one time, many have moved well beyond the notion of a handful of works hanging along a corridor to carefully conceived exhibitions - some actually housed in 'mini-Drumcroons' within the schools.

"There are 11 artists at schools throughout the Borough who both teach and do their own work; some are entering their third or fourth year of artist-in-residency. At the same time there is an artist-in-residence with studio at the Turnpike and an Art teacher on sabbatical doing his or her own art at Drumcroon.

Over the past fortnight those 11 artists-in-residence (in schools) have been joined by 35 printmakers from Manchester Polytechnic, working with an age range from five (primary) up to sixth form college where students can be 19. Then three well-known artists who are also printmakers - Patrick Hughes, Brendan Neiland and Michael Rothenstein - took up residence for a week, making prints."

These three artists were in residence at Drumcroon, while the Turnpike Gallery was "host to a marvellous selection of prints by Tom Phillips - with three workshop visits daily from schools". At the same time in the Derby Room (in the same building) the two printmakers in the Scheme, Carl Rowe and Adam Piper, were "also having big exhibitions". Drumcroon, too, was averaging three groups a day, and the exhibiting artist, Geoff Brunell, was in residence. In his capacity as a Fine Print lecturer, he had taught all the participating students and so his active involvement was central to the whole venture.

Artists-in-residence at Drumcroon

From the day Drumcroon opened a high priority has always been engaging children directly with established artists. In seeing artistic processes unfold before their eyes or over a comprehensible timespan, the visual arts can come alive in heightened and unexpected ways. Drumcroon has used the skills of a variety of artists in a variety of ways. The longest serving is Frank Egerton, who has had a studio in the Centre since 1983.

His studio has always been a favourite with visitors of all ages; his toys appeal to adults and children. His main tools (stanley and scalpel knives plus an extensive supply of sandpaper) surprise the more traditional craft, design and technology teacher, emphasising the significance of ideas and their realisation by the most appropriate means, as opposed to work stations and equipment determining the nature and sequence of activities, often to the point of concoction. The Schools Loan examples which surround him, as well as the work in hand, bear witness to an inventive and ingenious mind matched by special skills.

A cross-legged cat sprawled in an armchair, meticulously finished with a shiny paint surface, looks suspiciously like its maker - his animals reveal him as being an acute observer of human behaviour. A cumbersome hippo in boldly patterned attire pirhouettes daintily on a trapeze and a procession of animal pairs enters a Noah's Ark above which sits God, a zig-zag shaped flash of perspex lightning in one hand and a red watering can in the other, literally raining down cats and dogs. His first major work at Drumcroon, 'Wigan Wave', has a multi-coloured set of wooden waves as a main feature. Attached to them are richly painted and variously shaped fish, while against and above the two-toned mirror which doubles as sky, glide, swoop and dart a variety of seabirds. Some of his pieces can be operated: pull a foot and a mouth will open to reveal a small cat.

Egerton's wide knowledge of designing in general and in wood in particular has served the Centre well in other ways. He chose the furniture, musical instruments, carvings, toys and automata etc, which comprised the popular 'Wood' exhibition, while a comprehensive survey of his output was a highlight of the 1989 calendar at the Turnpike. A rare touring exhibition to come to Drumcroon was the 'Circus Comes to Town', chosen because he featured in it and arranged so that visitors could move easily between his studio and exhibits. Young visitors who naturally ask about skills and techniques when visiting his studio became enthralled by the content of his works and his knowledge of and attitudes towards the circus within the exhibition context.

Art teachers on sabbatical at Drumcroon

Vaizey made reference to an 'Art teacher on sabbatical'. A teacher has been seconded annually to work as an artist in Drumcroon (for a year) since the Centre opened - a unique innovation, to the best of our knowledge. To conclude the residency, each teacher exhibits in the Centre's galleries. The opportunity to immerse themselves in their work and contribute to the educational life of the Centre can prove regenerative according to Ken Cottam, the 1986-87 incumbent,

"As an artist I think the benefits have been tremendous because since leaving college I have never had the time to work in such a concentrated fashion. When you're painting at home you have your disciplined hour and a half on Sunday...It's so precious and it's such a small time that you feel everything you do has to count. So you tend to produce work which looks satisfactory in some way and you play safe...Because you haven't got the time for continuity of thought, you can't make those leaps which do occur in one's work." (4)

Working within this educational setting at Drumcroon

he inevitably became involved with visitors of all ages, which affected both his attitude and the progress of his work.

"Because of the nature of the establishment you're continually being questioned by children and students, 'What are you doing, why are you doing it?' When you try to explain to them, you have to explain it to yourself and in doing so you question what you're doing. As a teacher I've questioned what I'm doing in my work - the way I paint and the explanations I've made. I'm sure that must benefit me directly. This must have an effect on the way I approach teaching."

For Heather Macarty, the 1984-85 teacher-artist, the wealth of resources housed within Drumcroon richly benefited her work,

"Early in her residency she found inspiration in the Drumcroon library and an 'interest in Islamic patterns, Indian, Chinese and Primitive Art began to emerge and influence my work. This became apparent in the colour combinations of fabrics, threads and beaded patterns. I worked on small complex panels and further embellished their surface with plaiting and beading attached to the machine embroidery. The work involved methods which I had previously used, but these were now combined in a way that offered endless possibilities and created the intricate patterns and detailed textures strived for but never quite achieved on the surface of the parasols'." (5)

Her previous work involved re-covering old umbrellas and decorating the new surfaces. Reflecting on the residency, Heather was conscious that without the year

"...I might have continued without making my specialist subject an integral part of my art teaching. This would have left a gap in my experiences and in those I teach. The Artists in Wigan Schools Scheme has shown me how valuable a specialism should be especially when supported by the resources, art library, picture loan scheme and gallery services which are offered at this unique Centre."

The next year at Drumcroon, 1985-86, Carolyn Felton (who taught in a secondary school) went into one of its feeder primary schools; later on she went to the tertiary college to which many of the pupils from her 11-16 secondary school proceeded. This gave her an invaluable overview of the 5-19 con-

(Top) Michael Rothenstein surrounded by children during his 1983 exhibition of abstract prints of the sixties.

Six years on, Rothenstein returns to 'Past and Present'. Early childhood bird studies flank a work which they influenced 70 years later, and the children's related workshop work is spread out on the floor.

tinuum to which her secondary school practice contributed.

Already possessing the vital communication skills of the teacher, the majority who have worked in Drumcroon to date indicate that, when given the necessary space, they are able to build upon college and subsequent achievements. This combination of skills ensures that invaluable interactions take place with the many types of visitors who visit Drumcroon.

Exhibitions and short-term residencies at Drumcroon

Short-term residencies, in relation to the exhibited works, have always been a feature of the Drumcroon service. 'Past and Present' in January 1989 juxtaposed Michael Rothenstein's childhood works with his recent paintings and woodcuts, covering a 76-year span! During his visit he gave a talk to teachers which was attended by Sarah, an A-level student. She was then the holder of the Saturday morning post at Drumcroon, assisting visitors: she needed therefore to make herself fully conversant with the exhibition.

In writing about Rothenstein's painting of the London Underground, 'Going Home', in an A-level 'mock' examination, Sarah revealed the privileged information gleaned from meeting the artist. The artist expresses concern about the way advertisements play on both our fears and desires. "So many show disasters: images of guns pointed at our heads, images of threat, images of violence." Sarah relates this to the subliminal advertising practised in the States in the 1950s and then continues,

"...Rothenstein reassures himself of the existence of security in such an insecure and even dangerous environment by the inclusion of things which represent security and comfort to him - for instance a cigarette at the end of a day, a beautiful woman, and a brightly burning lamp. These things are arranged to one side of the work, many of them in collage - in fact, the whole work is made up of smaller pieces of paper, painted with acrylic and gouache. To the top of the work (there is no depth in the conventional sense) is a queue of people, like those entering or leaving the tube station, all of them anonymous, and at the bottom is a despatch rider with some outrageous neon-lights on his bike...He has a love of beautiful, bright colours, and these 'jewel-like' colours appear in the red of the underground sign, the orange glow of the cigarettes. I find Rothenstein's work very exciting." (6)

Sarah's 'inside knowledge', besides standing her in good stead in an examination, shows evidence of the artist stimulating her to study the work with intensity and increased awareness.

Michael Rothenstein's 'Past and Present' exhibition arose because the artist had donated to the Centre his entire collection of childhood works (1912-1925). Following the impact Drumcroon had made on him during his visits to his 1983 exhibition, he looked afresh at those earlier works after more than a 20-year interval.

"On seeing the drawings again, he discerned qualities which had been constant elements in all his subsequent works: particular shades of scarlet and blues, a use of contours and the 'particular way that forms jump and meet each other...It's all to do with energy and tracing the source of that energy - right back to source. It was a wonderful thing when you came along and made me look at this stuff'." (7)

Established artists often complain about the anonymity of the 'gallery circuit', in contrast it is the eager young children in Drumcroon who affect many artists through the warmth they generate. Rothenstein loves Drumcroon

"...and everything it stands for because of 'the feeling of freedom in the way the work is shown and the way everybody is going to receive the work'. This creates an 'open, flexible situation between the work and the people', and he has 'this feeling that we are in a business together which is deeply exciting and is a wonderful release'."

He admires the ways Drumcroon deals with the exhibited works - involving the artist, stimulating intensive discussion and related workshop activity, using slide and video material and, of course, the

Student visitors absorbed in the study of Isobel Smith's sketch and idea books during the 1988 'Connections' exhibition.

carefully presented books in conjunction with the works. He describes the multi-faceted approach as "the wrap around experience".

It is rare not to find the work of Wigan pupils contributing to the exhibitions. The teenage drawings of Rothenstein, with their strong linear qualities, lent themselves to photocopying. These accompanied the teachers' notes to schools, distributed many months in advance in order to allow for related practical work to be produced in schools. A resulting sequence of sixth form student work was displayed during 'Past and Present', with individuals picking up on particular features - the linear qualities, the autobiographical dimension, telling a story through sequence, the use of caricature, etc. Finally, the 'twinning' with the Turnpike gave rise to a shared catalogue, with that gallery showing Rothenstein's woodcuts of the 1980s.

How the 'Fragments' exhibition was constructed

Amongst longer-term residencies, that of the experimental print and papermaker Elizabeth Stuart Smith was made possible through a six-month North West Arts Fellowship. The exhibition catalogue at the conclusion of her residency recorded that

"...she has introduced many Wigan children to the mysteries of papermaking...'I think it has been quite a revelation to me to work with children and to enjoy it so much, because I really have enjoyed it'." (8)

In response to the 1983 Rothenstein exhibition's 1960s prints, in which he exploited the wood grains and textures of natural irregular surfaces, she saw affinities with her own approaches of pulping plants to make paper in the Japanese tradition.

"... I was working in a rather predatory way on the landscape. I'd go out, see a clump of cow parsley, and I'd think, 'Right, I'll have you. I'll make some paper out of you!' I'd go back again with my secateurs, cut it down, chop it up and turn it directly into a piece of work."

Her formal approach eventually gave way to involving countless young people in making paper and using it as a printmaking surface. Pupils became captivated by the whole business, which, in turn, led to further activities in schools, as the ten year-old Joanne makes clear,

"...the pulp felt just like thin porridge. We have started to make some pulp back at school, one with brown envelopes and one with newspaper and paper towels. The one with brown envelopes is going alright but the paper towels won't break down, they just stay in one piece unless you pick each one out and rip it up into tiny pieces. We have been using a potato masher and a whisk to break the paper up. We have got a pair of deckles out of the teachers' papermaking kit. For dyeing the pulp, Corrie brought some beetroot juice in. We were told to bring in some paper, a pot towel and anything we thought that would mix in..." (9)

The learning experiences opened up through Elizabeth's residency are commensurate with some of the requirements proposed for Technology in the National Curriculum, as well as furthering artistic understanding and awareness.

During the Spring Term of 1989 Elizabeth returned to the Centre to run a week of papermaking workshops for schools. These had a profound influence on Sylvia Watts, the 1988-89 seconded teacher-artist. A textiles artist, she had always wanted to work in paper but felt unable to take the first step "...until Elizabeth came in and made it seem so inviting and achievable." (10) Now, with the production of handmade papers incorporating dried flowers, leaves and inlaid threads she has been able to exercise even greater control of materials.

Sylvia's exhibition at the end of her year's secondment was called 'Fragments'; its conception and construction provides further evidence of the multi-faceted approach which so appeals to Rothenstein. It also reveals the complex ways in which artists contribute to practice throughout the Authority as well as participating in specific residencies; each of the other exhibitors related to Sylvia and her work.

Elizabeth was invited to display some of her work as a matter of course, and her paperworks occupied the Small Gallery at Drumcroon. Sue Peterson, who had joined the Artists in Wigan Schools Scheme in 1987, worked (on her first placement) with Sylvia Watts at Cansfield High where she taught Art. Sue commented on Sylvia's attractive teaching area, "...its wonderful arrangements encouraged me to take on board the drawing of aged objects...I love the way museum objects are stored in a different context, there's a kind of preciousness about the way they're displayed". This preciousness manifests itself in her work for she sets the most delicate textiles constructions into plaster and they suggest freshly made archaeological or geological discoveries. Sylvia says, "Sue came in with a totally different kind of work and that extended what I was able to do with the children." It was natural, therefore, to include Sue's works, which occupied the Coffee Lounge.

Sylvia's textiles and paperworks occupied the walls of the Main Gallery, their richness and quality bearing testimony to her industry and commitment throughout the year. Her studio was always stimulating, as is her school-based teaching area, and her skills in demonstrating the stimulus material in relation to her work through attractive arrangements was carried through into the gallery. Beautiful shells, a shallow basket of stones, dried flower heads and photographs of textural surfaces in nature looked especially effective occupying a fireplace area, for example. The week she began her residency, so did Clare Leaver who worked for a short while as a ceramicist in an outbuilding. She left because her travel costs were too high but was invited to contribute to 'Fragments'. Her ceramic sculptures of architectural forms complemented to perfection Sylvia's work in the Main Gallery. Kelly, a fifth form Work Experience pupil, interviewed Clare, and the written piece which resulted now accompanies the Schools Loan examples of Clare's work.

"In her workshop Clare has some outstanding pieces of work all based on the topic of 'old buildings'. When I first went to see Clare's work I got a cold feeling, an outside feeling and I practically expected grass to start sprouting around the base of the columns. The 'old buildings' idea began in her third year at Manchester Polytechnic. 'I started on a piece that would express my feelings about walking into an abbey so I used some qualities like rubble, texture and coarse areas and it was really spontaneous. Then I started to concentrate more on the columns using them in a way that would suggest what an abbey was all about...' She won't make pieces to someone else's design. But she would like to work on a larger scale...Having enjoyed the smaller pieces so much, I would love one day to come across a large sculptural piece by Clare." (11)

Kelly illustrates that the pupil, too, can make effective use of the content, form, process, mood model; it provided her with a structure to interview Clare, transcribe and write about her and her work.

Another important dimension of 'Fragments' was the basement area given over to the first year teacher who took Sylvia's place at Cansfield for the year. She was invited to display her pupils' work and was exhilarated by the invaluable experience of being able to see and appraise the work in a gallery context - the quality, quantity, rich colour and variety of

Melanie Young's sketchbooks, painting props and postcards lead on to two bold 'My Body' project portraits by primary pupils.

Norma Tait's use of the same space in 'Connections' illustrates how the 'Ripple Model' uses content, form, process and mood to literally lead to other places and cultures.

'Drumcroon has been incredibly useful as my wood carving came from inspiration after visiting and viewing the work of Frank Egerton,' wrote Philip: the resulting car on display in his 1990 A-level exhibition.

▲ Frank Egerton's Schools Loan Collection 'Strong Man' is a popular item which is frequently on display in his Drumcroon studio.

Sylvia Watts' Drumcroon studio during her 1988-89 residency year.

work took her aback! A range of the pupils' work related to that of Joyce Marney, a textiles designer who had been tempted to set up studio in the Cansfield Art and Design department while she was between jobs. The unusual initiative shown by the young teacher in so utilising the skills of this artist added an enriching dimension to 'Fragments'.

In the upstairs Conference Room, further examples of pupil work were to be discovered. Coloured panels constructed with mathematical implications, based on the study of ethnic objects from the Schools Loan Collection had been made by St Andrew's Primary School pupils when Sylvia undertook a short residency there. (These are now in the Wigan Children's Library, for which they were designed, as are a set made at Stubshaw Cross Primary School with Isobel Smith, also featured in the Conference Room.) Paperworks by Golborne Comprehensive pupils and textiles pieces from Hesketh Fletcher High School indicated something of the breadth of activity now possible at the GCSE level.

The main wall of the Conference Room was given over to the textiles works of two Winstanley Sixth Form College students, Caroline and Renu, who had spent a week at Drumcroon working along-

▲ Clare Leaver's ceramic architectural sculptures were an important feature of 'Fragments'.

A section of the Main Gallery during the 1989 'Fragments' exhibition.

side Sylvia. A wealth of sketchbook and investigative research indicated the rigour underpinning their course. Renu's work drew extensively on Indian forms and symbols. One item was a beautifully designed small bag incorporating a peacock feather, symbolising an Indian god and the religious faith of her mother (for whom it was made), with the rich yellow and cerise reflecting the mother's favourite sari colours. This gave rise to her mother performing a fashion display of her saris and jewellery to the accompaniment of Indian music - a session described by one observer as being 'quite entrancing'. For all its variety, the 'Fragments' exhibition added up to a cohesive whole reflecting the interactive critical studies approaches developed in Wigan.

Centre staff, artists, teachers and students worked closely together in its creation, in keeping with the partnership principles which recur throughout this book. To reflect further on Drumcroon while looking to the chapters ahead with their school-based emphasis, let us conclude this section with the words of a primary deputy head teacher in her documentation of her pupils use of the Amanda Faulkner exhibition:

"A Working Partnership: School - Artist - Gallery
Through this partnership a richness was possible that otherwise could have been elusive.

Many of the steps taken were tentative, the results precious...Surely the 'My Body' science project must somewhere be about making self-connections, be about exploring, drawing out and making connections with hidden, inner selves, physically and mentally. Drumcroon, with the Amanda Faulkner exhibition, offered a wonderful extension to this. Children and adults sharing a viewing and reading of the work. All of us making our own self-connections.

The exhibition and the work undertaken with the 'My Body' project provided a context for the testing and challenging of attitudes and social values that should not be avoided." (12)

The Artists in Wigan Schools: Beginnings

2

"During the eight months of unemployment (1983-84) I had endured prior to starting at Abraham Guest High School my work had suffered due to a lack of space and incentive, mainly due to the very limited contact I had with other artists or people who were interested in what I was trying to do. For several months I stopped working completely." (1)

Tadek Beutlich Schools Loan hangings and carefully displayed magazine and book material in a corner of Angela Cusani's Golborne Comprehensive studio.

The first 'Artists in Wigan Schools' exhibition. Circular cushion covers and dress by Eram, the works to the left of Angela's large paperwork by Barbara, a fifth form pupil.

In order to find out which young artists seeking employment were living in Wigan, I obtained lists from the two tertiary and two sixth form institutions in the Authority. From these it was possible to identify which students should have graduated in Art and Design the previous July, assuming they had continued their education without having time out.

By following up those with a telephone number, I identified ten well-qualified unemployed young artists who had returned home to Wigan. Through lack of facilities, resources, finances and incentive a considerable reservoir of talent was clearly going to waste. Here, surely, was a potential workforce capable of making an impact on Wigan's schools in keeping with the Entitlement Policy and the Principles underpinning Drumcroon. In the process, the artists would benefit and, as many of them had themselves been educated in Wigan, an unusual continuity would be established.

An application was made to the Manpower Services Commission (MSC) with a view to harnessing the skills of ten artists for a year. (2) The application considered the implications for both the artists and the local community. The "benefits to artists, all with potential employment implications" arising out of working in schools were listed as follows:

1) The incentive to continue and develop their work, whereas many cease to practise because of lack of opportunities in the years after graduation.

2) Substantial portfolios could lead on to exhibitions, further training or art-related employment.

3) Most would be applying their skills for the benefit of others for the first time in genuine practical contexts.

4) Using appropriate language to communicate with others about art would develop a valuable new skill in many.

5) This process could aid their evaluation and understanding of their own work.

6) Applying hitherto 'private' skills to the needs of others could lead to personal growth and social confidence.

7) They could become better equipped to secure other community posts as artists working in galleries, hospitals, factories, other schools, etc.

Eight possible benefits to both schools and the wider community were likewise set out. These were:

1) Pupils' increased understanding of artists' ideas and working methods would make the visual arts more interesting and accessible to them.

2) They would be able to see how an artist's work proceeds and develops over a period of time.

3) Through discussion with artists, the discipline involved in making art would become apparent.

4) The unusual stimulus would enable teachers to extend considerably what is normally on offer.

5) Artists' work and displays would appreciably affect the school environment.

6) Their presence should cause the pupils' work to develop in new and significant directions.

7) Especially in a community school setting, adults as well as pupils could benefit.

Six years on: Barbara with her first post-degree work in the 'Drumcroon: the First Ten Years' exhibition, 1990-91.

8) The high school and related primary school links should aid continuity by developing closer liaison and understanding.

A residency in every high school, with the addition of each high school having a link with four feeder primary schools, could involve a total of 100 schools over a year. An attempt was made to identify the range of potential benefits, but with hindsight, knowing the full impact artists have had on schools, the benefits as set out were remarkably understated. In the event the MSC rejected the submission on the grounds that it would "benefit the individual artist more than the community". Fortunately, Wigan's Director of Education agreed to the funding of three artists, and so the Artists in Wigan Schools Scheme was born, albeit in a less ambitious form. The three young artists, Gillian Travers, Anne-Marie Quinn and Angela Cusani, set up studios in three secondary school Art and Design departments, beginning their work as resident artists in September 1984. Given that MSC response, it is interesting that 15 months later Marina Vaizey felt able to write,

"The Wigan initiative is in the long run the best thing for artists, encouraging the whole community to think visually...The basis should be in schools and colleges, and the hard slog of providing throughout the country ways and means of art meeting the public." (3)

The first recruits working in a secondary school

Unemployment was at its worst during the 1983-84 period Gillian Travers was on the dole after obtaining a First Class BA Honours degree in Textiles. Like Gillian, Anne-Marie Quinn experienced the traumas of unemployment and of attempting to work in isolation. She started out with 'hopeful' ideas of continuing her work,

"But as the year went on my motivation dwindled. I found it a terrific struggle to draw, and at the end of a day of producing nothing I hated myself and my confidence went. I became very low, calling myself an artist without working. I hardly had any communication with other artists or saw exhibitions, and I think I turned in on myself." (4)

Anne-Marie still works in the Scheme: she now has extensive experience working with pupils of all ages and abilities in all categories of schools. As will be seen in the next section, her own work continues to develop significantly and her influence has been considerable because of her special communication skills. With a new-found belief in her talents, Gillian's work also blossomed and Abraham Guest High School benefited to such a degree from the stimulus

Gillian Travers' Abraham Guest school studio: a pupil making connections between the design and ideas stages and completed works.

Work from Gillian Travers' Abraham Guest school residency filled the Drumcroon Small Gallery in the 'Artists in Wigan Schools' exhibition.

Gillian Travers' residency work: Schools Loan Lynne Moore card prints, block and supporting information, and a Matisse book acknowledging his influence on both artists.

she provided that some of the directions the school work was taking over a year later could be traced back to her residency. After six months she was appointed as a designer to work for Laura Ashley - her residency work caused considerable interest at the interview.

Gillian was replaced by a sculptor, Andy Shaw. Having 'run out of steam' working alone on the dole using a shed at the bottom of the garden, he had already been working for a short period, unpaid, in a Drumcroon outbuilding. Although having reservations about joining the Scheme, in time he proved himself to be an exceptional communicator. Along with Angela Cusani, who joined the Scheme straight from her degree year and therefore did not have to experience unemployment, these four artists rapidly made an impact in Wigan during that first year. The obvious value they brought to schools made it doubly regrettable that the MSC did not see fit to enable those other unemployed artists to have similar opportunities.

The MSC submission was not wasted: its content became the basis for an unofficial contract between artist, school and authority and it was three years before it needed any redrafting. The main principles were tested in residency after residency and contributed to the working partnerships between teachers and artists which have become central to the Scheme. Firstly, the 50/50 principle taken from the MSC submission ensured that the artists' time was divided more or less equally between the development of their own work and the practical needs of the young people they worked with. The principle sought to bring together the best the author had observed in other residencies: in some, young people observed an artist at work and had opportunities to ask questions, while in others, the artist would introduce a project, usually related to the themes or processes in his or her own work, which the children would carry out. In one the children were passive, learning about an artist's concepts and working methods. In the other, the children were practically involved, with the artist's own work providing only a generalised backcloth - the artist often merely holding up examples as illustrations. In the event, all manner of relationships and connections between artists' and pupils' work emerged.

The second principle required the school to provide a studio space for the artist, and for the artist to make this both attractive and informative. The Golborne Comprehensive head of Art and Design describes Angela Cusani's work space and her ability to establish relationships.

"Angela transformed a rather dull corner of the Art room into a riot of colour almost overnight, and this area was to grow in its richness and quality during the year. Colour suddenly became three-dimensional, the rich and seductive quality of which was so delightful and attractive that it was impossible to pass Angela's area without being enticed to take a closer look." (5)

"Her area became a focal point for anyone and everyone who came to the Art room. Whatever the visit, a group of small children from the feeder primary schools, some friendless pupil with nothing to do in the lunch-time, the headmaster on his round with the School Governors, some visiting student or lecturer - the reception was always the same - a lovely smile and welcome, a gleam in the eye and the ability to communicate on whatever level, giving a charming account of her work, its inspiration and the fascinating techniques she employs. She became an immediate hit with all the children and groups she worked with."

It was fitting that Gillian Travers went to work for Laura Ashley. The textiles approaches she introduced at Abraham Guest affected the pupils so profoundly that the residency culminated in a bold and imaginative Fashion Show in the school. Younger pupils had come every lunch-time to design and make colourful batik blouses, all the hems willingly hand or machine sewn at home. Gillian's allied use of Schools Loan non-precious jewellery led to pupils making necklaces, earrings and bracelets - to enhance the blouses they had made.

Artist and head of department had worked closely on a second year project which led to pupils designing and making outfits and accessories for their friends, a project which in turn led to face-painting and body adornment. The head of department recorded that,

"Gillian's work expresses a real enjoyment of colour, her ideas being realised in a variety of media, including tempera, dye, ink and print on various surfaces. The pupils had the experience of seeing colour used as an integral part of organisations or design, but not only on a painted or modelled surface - a deepening understanding of materials having their own local colour. In practice this was to lead to the Garment and Jewellery Project adopted and made entirely possible by the enthusiasm of 1st and 2nd year pupils." (6)

At Cardinal Newman High School, Anne-Marie's use of the human figure as the main motif in her

23

pastel paintings was complemented by a variety of means whereby every year in the school became involved in intense study of the figure. There was no shortage of offers from pupils to take turns in posing, for Anne-Marie brought in a variety of dresses for the purpose and created appropriate settings in which to place the model. In order to reach a wider audience she spent the final stages of the residency working in the school foyer with pupils working alongside her. The area was transformed by an exhibition of her work and the school's pupils, as well as work from the primary schools in which she had worked. In consequence, there were studies of the figure by infant children through to 16 year-olds as well as her own. In addition, the theme of the nude in art led to an accompanying display of large reproductions of the subject by Degas, Manet, Botticelli, Matisse and Picasso. Anne-Marie was adept at arousing in young people an interest in the artists to whom she, too, was responsive. The head of department wrote,

Donna, a fifth form pupil, working in the Cardinal Newman school main entrance area, converted into a gallery and studio during Anne-Marie Quinn's residency.

Primary cray-pas paintings and secondary figure drawings, displayed in Drumcroon, illustrate the skills which Anne-Marie develops in pupils.

"Certainly the exhibitions of work which Anne-Marie made uniquely her own, supported by illustrations, books and so forth would have been unlikely to have arisen without her presence." (7)

Residencies in primary schools

The artists obviously had to establish themselves in the secondary school before taking on the shorter-term primary residencies. Besides the quality of experience which this brought to younger pupils, the Scheme also proved an invaluable liaison exercise, extending to primary head teachers and secondary school deputies with liaison responsibilities. It also generated movement between pupils and staff in non-threatening ways because of the neutral role of the artist; the links were real and tangible.

Having hesitated about joining the Scheme, Andy Shaw continued to work at Drumcroon, engaging with children there. Later he agreed to undertake a three-week residency in a school: if the reaction was favourable there would be a place for him the next year. In the event, every child at Wigan St Patrick's Primary School had drawn from a live dog in advance of him starting there. These drawings acted as the basis for a set of stunning sculptures produced by the infants, and Andy is still working within the Scheme.

The first 'Artists in Wigan Schools' exhibition, 1985

In September 1985, Drumcroon staged the first 'Artists in Wigan Schools' exhibition, bringing together the work of all four artists and that of young people resulting from the artists residencies in schools. The artists helped to set up the exhibition, their brief being to recreate the nature, appearance and spirit - as far as was feasible - of their school-based environments and displays. They fulfilled this brief admirably. This exhibition affected so many visitors that it is worth quoting one high school head of department from a neighbouring authority who was a regular visitor to Drumcroon.

"I found the whole experience overwhelming. I went from room to room and I felt that the whole thing was so powerful. The evidence of commitment on the part of both the artists and the pupils who had been fortunate enough to come into contact with them came together to create something that I, as a school teacher, felt it was impossible to cope with or compete with. I was

aware of an energy and a force that I don't think you see from even the best school departments. It was the extra input of somebody being single-minded about the things that they cared about and pursuing and communicating those interests to children that left me feeling totally and utterly drained after about 15 minutes." (8)

Following their school fashion show, the Abraham Guest High School pupils agreed to participate in the Drumcroon preview, making the Small Gallery where

A second year participant in the fashion show at the end of the residency.

(Far left) Jane, a first year pupil, wearing the batik blouse she has made and Schools Loan non-precious jewellery.

Jane, now an A-level student, wearing the felt and bead headpiece she has made. (It has matching belt, anklets and purse.)

their work and Gillian's was displayed the venue for another unusual feature of the evening.

"The place was absolutely packed and buzzing and as I turned into one room, there were these young children decorating their faces, totally confident about what they were doing...I've seen young children getting ready for performances and being self-conscious, showing off, or being silly. These children were just so sure about what they were doing that the fact that there were all these adults around them, with glasses of wine, just didn't affect them at all. They were totally

This sketchbook design of a second year pupil, Mandy, by her friend was made for the fashion project.

Mandy as she appeared during the fashion project.

Mandy showing off the whole outfit.

Infants at work on their dog sculptures at St Patrick's Primary School with a Schools Loan sculpture by Andy Shaw in the foreground.

She had cried every day since starting school, but stopped the day she began sculpting her dog.

When Andy started his St Patrick's residency he discovered that every child had already made studies from actual dogs: this drawing is by a four year-old.

(Middle Above) The influence of Raymond's dog drawing on his sculpture is unmistakeable.

Every infant's sculpture had character: their dogs displayed during the first Drumcroon 'Artists in Wigan Schools' exhibition, 1985.

concerned about presenting themselves in as professional (though maybe that's not quite the right word) a way as they could, because they obviously cared so much about what had happened to them through doing this. They were so proud of helping one another - and the teamwork!"

Outside the Small Gallery the visitor was confronted by a boldly coloured woven structure extending up two floors, attached to the bannister rails. Each artist was in residence in the Centre during the course of the exhibition, and primary children had constructed this piece working with Angela Cusani during the first week which culminated in the Preview.

Angela and Anne-Marie shared the Main Gallery, their work combining to form one rich whole. Angela's main piece was a large handmade paper work built out of coloured paper lengths on a weft-warp basis. Each length was worked into and decoratively embellished, the whole 'lifted' by fluorescent notes of colour. Barbara's adjacently hung construction (by a fifth former) was a variant with alternating woven and satin strips, the latter dyed at home. Interestingly, this was completed well in advance of that by Angela, its format being determined by Barbara's understanding of what the artist was about as opposed to being an imitation of a product. The visiting head of department said,

"If I am being honest, because the artists hadn't had any teacher training I expected there to be gaps and weaknesses and things that were brave attempts but hadn't quite come off, and I found the quality of the work very, very impressive. It struck me that it had to be something to do with the fact that these artists were so committed themselves. They didn't see themselves as teaching something or building something over five years, or having total responsibility for a programme of work. They were there to exchange, explore and to probably find out for themselves - it was crusading!"

What he focuses on is extremely important. For good reasons teachers seek to build coherent courses for their pupils which are often 'incremental'. Through partnership with the artist, what is on offer is imbued with an extra vitality and excitement outside normal 'school art'. Even if the course logic is temporarily upset, the added richness more than compensates. If the course is built on sound principles, the new dimensions introduced by the artist can be built upon after the residence. In *Educating for Art,* the 'illuminating experiences' demonstrate how the attitudes of young people can be dramatically changed: these artists affected many young people and their levels of motivation. The art educator, too, can be similarly affected: the visitor found the experience so overwhelming that he literally had to go out into the street to compose himself.

"I went back in again and started to pick a way through that overwhelming impression. I tried to shut out a lot and concentrate on an individual piece or a group of works. I found the standard then got more and more impressive because I started to realise that there were thought processes behind the work that were very, very powerful. It wasn't entertainment for the children, it wasn't novelty value. You felt that some of these children would go on and develop - some of them, I'm sure - along lines that were instigated by the artists. The actual experience of coming into contact with somebody practising their skills and interests will have changed them. You could see that in the work."

There were countless outstanding pupil achievements in evidence: in the woven and knitted dress by Eram (9) she had brought together European and Asian values for the very first time. Four cibachrome photographs of her wearing this dress against a background of one of Angela's weavings brought it, and the interactive process with the artist, vividly to life. Donna's cray-pas paintings adorned a chimney breast wall, and each infant's sculpted dog was worthy of study.

One extraordinary pupil achievement was the dog sculpture and studies by Dale, aged ten. Andy had never visited Dale's school, but Dale had met and talked to Andy at Drumcroon. A quite brilliant sequence of ambitious dog studies had resulted, finally giving rise to a clay sculpture of a lying dog built onto a chicken wire base. His accompanying statement explained that it had taken him "about 176 hours" in all, and boot polish had been used to stain its back black. Cracks appeared, but had been worked together with a vinegar and water mixture. Some months later his mother phoned Drumcroon - the cracks had got worse. It was too late: the dog is now no more. As a result he came to Saturday morning classes at Drumcroon, working with Andy. Two

A PGCE student's third term assignment exhibition influenced by the Wigan residency scheme.

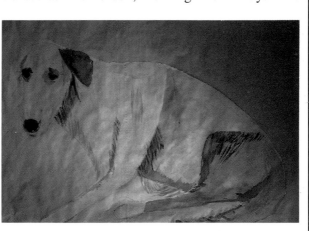

Dale, age ten, made a series of superb dog studies following his meeting with Andy at Drumcroon in 1985.

Dale's dog sculpture was built in clay over a chicken wire base: he stained its back with boot polish and it took 'about 176 hours' in all!

2.22 Two years on: Dale making a dog during Saturday morning classes at Drumcroon. The dog was displayed in the family's lounge.

years later he could be seen rounding off a four foot high standing dog, a sculpture which went on to adorn the family lounge. The power of the 'illuminating experience'!

The visitor to this particular exhibition was on secondment from his head of department post as a Postgraduate Certificate of Education (PGCE) lecturer at Manchester.

"Being on the PGCE course this year with the responsibility of preparing student-teachers for a career in schools, and feeling not as well-read and not as well-researched as the resident tutors, that exhibition - more than anything else - has given me the confidence to approach the preparation of students by getting them to work to their strengths. They have got very recent, and hopefully intense, experience of producing work. That is probably the great advantage that they have got over experienced teachers who know their pupils and their schools very well. Working from their strengths can give them an insight which goes way beyond exercises and the normal tricks of the trade."

But for having visited that exhibition, he does not think that he would have had the confidence to encourage students to push so hard for what they believe and care about in their interactions with pupils. He would probably have been saying, "You have got to offer a wide range" out of a fear of otherwise selling them short.

The third term curriculum PGCE assignment was a new course initiative. His students "looked long and hard" at the concept of artists in schools and whether they might gain further insight into their teaching practice performances by operating outside the normal student-teacher situation, reconciling their BA Honours practical skills with their brief as trainee teachers to communicate.

"One of the PGCE students has actually been in my own school department and has changed four or five pupils overnight by working in a very expressive way with batik. The work of two or three fifth formers has changed radically, one of them as a result of half an hour's conversation with that student who was producing work she really cared about. I know that lad and his work and have seen what happened. One girl, who was like water in your hand trying to keep hold of her and getting her to come back after school, came and produced four batiks in a week and it doubled her 16+ exhibition. She brought her parents in to see her work, which she would never have done if

she hadn't produced these batiks."

However, the student initially disclaimed the influence but the lecturer suggested that she compare the girl's batiks with any other work in the department then, "ask yourself if that end wall that is full of your work has had an impact on her or not!" He put the girl's work alongside that of the student, "and it was a very powerful connection". In just a short time the student brought wide-ranging benefits to the school and the pupils she worked with "loved the experience".

"And of course the juniors say, 'What is this? What's going on? What's happening? Can we go and talk to her? Can we have a look at what she's doing? Why is that wax melting? What's she doing with it? How's she got that effect?' An excitement that isn't generated by the regular work of the department!"

At the annual exhibition and open evening of the polytechnic PGCE course, the curriculum assignment display of the student's work alongside that of the pupils' batiks was a highlight. Three or four other displays demonstrated the impact the students had had upon pupils and the students talked of the value of interacting with young people, gaining insights over and above those gained on teaching practice. The effect of the first 'Artists in Wigan Schools' exhibition on one art educator illustrates that important features can be transferred with benefit.

Anne-Marie Quinn, Angela Cusani and Andy Shaw were keen to stay in the Wigan Scheme and the confidence they had gained meant that they made an immediate impact on a new school. They were joined by three more artists at the beginning of the second year of the Scheme through a successful application for funding to the Calouste Gulbenkian Foundation who were keen to complement the secondary school placements with residencies of an in-depth primary nature. Further funding from The Elephant Trust guaranteed that appropriate materials for the children's related practice could be introduced into these schools to further develop the 50/50 principle's implications.

3 Intimate Relationships

"delicate
thoughts flowing through my skin and blood
trying to reach a place where they can settle.
Things I hate on my body.
relationships
touching
hands holding their relationship together
legs appearing next to my body.
My ears listening to the rest of my body.
I hate wearing slippers.
Lost thoughts.
Hard and strong, but delicate.
My stomach is warm and gentle.
Things I like on my body.
Peeling back old to new skin.
Warmth of skin.
I hate the scar on my left arm.
Swirling scarves.
I feel great on the picture of my body.
I love the bit of blue in my eye.
Clothes touching.
I love the wind rushing over my body.
Skin holding me together.
Sun shines through my body." (1)

Junior pupils cray-pas studies made from life of a class mate posing in ballet outfit.

The 'My Body' project

Anne-Marie was resident for a month at Tyldesley County Primary School specifically in support of the 'My Body' project in which the school was involved. As it developed, the children worked to ever-deepening levels, using their own handmade paper. Anne-Marie wrote about Claire's resulting book,

"Words and ideas that were clarified yesterday and externalised, have now appeared in the paper book. Claire has followed the threads with a lot of her written ideas - linking to different parts of her body. That feels very satisfying - to actually make the connections like that, and draw it all together in her way, back and front, enjoying both her heavily worked tissue and paper 'front', as well as the almost accidental beauty of the back - the lovely qualities in the paper itself joined by raffia and thread, now with words. A joy!" (2)

As the project continued to unfold there were moments when Anne-Marie had to act with special sensitivity,

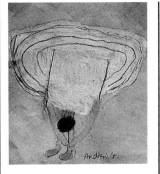

Claire, aged ten, gives expression to intimate feelings about her body following the visit her group made to the Amanda Faulkner exhibition at Drumcroon. The artist Anne-Marie Quinn accompanied them and on the return to school they made drawings of themselves. Claire's words are extracted from the drawing she made. Anne-Marie, too, had recently begun incorporating words into her collage works. But for this, she does not think that she would have had the confidence "to actually work on that with children - the word and the image".

"So now it comes to sharing this with the rest of the class, which I think is a vital part of the process - to share and pass on this enjoyment, this celebration of themselves which has been a very delicate, personal probing and peeling back. But it has to be done carefully - not to be intrusive - both 'parties' have to understand its importance." (3)

Properly handled, art experiences of this kind contribute to the personal and social education of young people. Nevertheless, Anne-Marie has worked in schools where involvement in 'My Body' remained at the level where "the classrooms have got big skeletons that the teachers have done with arrows pointing to different organs and things". Cross-curricular developments certainly took place in the secondary residencies during the first year of the Artists in Wigan Schools Scheme, but the primary sector provided natural environments and more conducive timetable structures for artists to become involved in projects across the curriculum.

The culmination of Anne-Marie's first major primary residency at Standish Lower Ground School was, however, a joyous celebration of the children's art achievements. Her own use of pastel and treatment of the figure was reflected in the ambitious work of the children, which featured large figures developed from studies based on posed colleagues and the bold use of cray-pas. Two other primary residencies within a short distance from Standish Lower Ground School reached their culmination at the same time, so the Drumcroon staff devised what they called 'A Children's Art Treasure Hunt' in the Spring term of 1986. Visitors were invited to go to the three schools along a three mile route. Each school invited parents to attend and groups of children were to be observed working alongside each artist throughout the evening.

'A Children's Art Treasure Hunt'

Two Yorkshire teachers made the 130 mile round trip: the experience of the evening suggested all sorts of implications for their own practice and locality.

"It surpassed my expectations because it gave me a vision of what could happen if it was properly organised in schools in my area...The art had taken over the schools, and that was so exciting to an artist. I tried to do that in my school, I tried to take over the school, and for a time I could make it work. But with those artists and the organisation behind them there was a lot of love there and, well, there was a threeway thing - there were the parents and there were the children and then the artists and the pictures. You could feel the communication was going on through the work and through the displays, but I didn't feel the displays were as important as actually seeing the children working and adding to the display." (4)

Having initially enjoyed observing children papermaking with Mary Connelly at school number one, Wigan St Andrew's, in "a stimulating, visually exciting environment", even though situated in "a

depressing sort of area, very built-up", they then went on to Standish Lower Ground,

"...and that looked even more depressing when we arrived. We picked our way through the potholes in the playground and we found this little door and opened it and 'Wham!' There was this picture zooming...The colour was amazing. When you came in from the dark outside there were people, and then the picture behind - and then there were the kids...the whole thing was together, just like you've always wanted it to be. I went away thinking that somehow or other this sort of structure is the most exciting thing I've seen in schools for a long time - or in colleges, for that matter."

The picture was a giant ballet frieze covering every conceivable wall space in the school entrance area. Some of the dancers depicted were two and three times the size of the pupils who had executed them, and the whole was in richly glowing cray-pas. Anne-Marie's medium of pastel had naturally led to the study of Degas' work and so to the theme of the ballet. During the course of the evening pupils were to be observed posing for their classmates dressed up in ballet outfits, just as they had done at a formative stage in the project.

"They had actually been posing, hadn't they! The children had been doing these very vital charcoal drawings of them...They'd just finished and they were all propped up on chairs. Beautiful little Picassoesque drawings. You compared them to other painters - but that directness and that boldness of vision! The little girls were full of it, being dressed up, and I said, 'Will you come and stand in front of the picture for us?' and nothing was too much trouble and they came and posed with their picture. What I felt, and the kids seemed to feel, was that they'd changed the school completely."

Two parents introduced themselves to the teachers, having overheard their animated conversation, but it soon became apparent that "they weren't aware that something special was going on!" They assumed that it was normal for young people to enjoy the opportunities on offer here.

"We said to them, 'Do you not realise how extraordinary this is, because in our area there is very little on this level in these sort of schools and there is no structure to back it up?' and they looked at us as though we were a bit deprived."

(Far eft) Vanessa's studies were used as a basis for an A1 pastel of a ballet dancer.

The recreation of the pose after Vanessa had completed her painting.

As the school was one of the last small village-types remaining in Wigan, the head teacher had been worried about Anne-Marie having satisfactory space to work in. There was, "no hall, no corridors, no spare room of any kind and this lack of space necessitated Anne-Marie's working in the class-room with children and teachers with only one space between two movable bookcases to call her own". Third and fourth year juniors also shared this space, but,

"In no way did this dampen her enthusiasm, which she transferred to the children, who quickly became competent in the use of pastels and learned much from Anne-Marie about colour, light and shade." (5)

One great advantage of working in such conditions was the possibility of directly involving every child in the school. The head teacher gathered children's observations on the completion of the residency. Besides the obvious sense of enjoyment and in-volvement in the activities, they also convey evidence of important learning experiences.

Anna (aged 11): *"It was nice to meet someone so interested in art. I enjoyed everything Anne-Marie did with us. I know exactly how to mix pastels because Anne-Marie showed me what to do."*

Pupils at work on the life-size chorus line section of the giant 'Ballet Frieze'.

On entering the school, 'there was this picture zooming everywhere. The colour was amazing'.

There was evidence of real learning in the boldness of scale, relationships of colour and figures, and in the treatment of form and tone.

The group project still allowed children to lose themselves in the making of art.

Christopher (aged 10): *"It was dead good having Anne-Marie in school. She taught me all about pastels and how to draw people - noses mostly, and mouths (I already knew about eyes). I can draw feet really well now and shade the*

An awareness of Japanese screens and of the art of Klimt and Bonnard is apparent in these panels by junior pupils.

Infants 'measuring' themselves against their mother and child panels on seeing them vertically displayed for the first time.

shapes of arms and positions of legs. Anne-Marie taught me how to use really bright colours."

Louise (aged 11): *"I feel I've become good at drawing because of Anne-Marie. I didn't used to be a good drawer but now I know how to draw people in different positions and how to smudge pastels with my thumb."*

Stuart (aged 7): *"It was good fun colouring with Anne-Marie. I used charcoal and pastels and I drew ballet dancers. She taught me how to draw dead nice and I showed our Andrew how to draw at home."*

Vanessa (aged 11): *"It was good having Anne-Marie in school. I've never used pastels like that before. Anne-Marie taught me all about light and shade, and I modelled for her in my ballet dress."*

John (aged 8): *"I thought it was good doing Art with Anne-Marie. I coloured the red dress on the big 'Ballet Frieze'. She showed me how to draw people better. I didn't know what violet was but Anne-Marie taught me what all the colours are called and I now know the names of all of them."*

A cray-pas rendering of a posed European mother and child by a Chinese pupil, Kidman, age ten.

The third school, involving Angela Cusani was equally impressive. The two visitors found that the whole evening "really was a treasure hunt because it was a treasure every time - it just unfolded". Because they had previously visited Drumcroon they "felt it

was bound to be good because of our confidence in the sub-structure - and also the title was intriguing, wasn't it!" They returned over the Pennines feeling the need of similar provision there.

"I keep hoping that some sort of structure can be produced in our area where we could get artists into schools in exactly the same sort of way - because I couldn't fault it, I kept on thinking, 'Well, what's the snag here?'"

Dating back to sixth form college days, Anne-Marie had used the female figure as the basis for virtually all her work, but at Standish this took a new direction. Her friend Tessa was expecting her first baby and posed for Anne-Marie, leading to a major sequence of collages and pastel paintings on the theme of the pregnant nude. The most ambitious in scale marked her next residency at Hindley County Primary. Anne-Marie wanted "to explore the mother and child with the children" in order to clearly relate their work to her own; this fitted in with the school's involvement in the national 'My Body' project.

'A Mother and Child' project

The head teacher organised a rota of local mothers and babies to pose for children from reception age upwards through the whole school, helped by a Pram Club which met regularly in the school. Anne-Marie gathered reference material, including mother and child reproductions: Japanese print examples and works by Mary Cassatt and Berthe Morisot inviting comparison with the traditional male treatment of the theme. The Advisory Teacher for Art (Primary) in her documentation of the project recorded that

"The children worked initially on small charcoal studies of the mothers and children and from these individual studies a series of large panels were begun. On long pieces of paper the children enlarged their images either individually or in groups. The children's use of cray-pas for these panels was greatly enriched through their observations of Anne-Marie at work." (6)

At the culmination of this residency, the works of both artist and children were shown to great advantage in Drumcroon's 'In the Round' exhibition. Though the larger panels could not be accommodated, A2 pastel paintings extended up the staircase with larger group works on the landing, leading into the Conference Room where the pregnant nude series formed an ethereal suite, to the pleasure of countless visitors and the obvious satisfaction of the artist.

"That is when it all comes together. That was nice, because you were led up the stairs by the work of the children to my work. That's like stopping and assessing what's gone on and then leading on from that. The Conference Room was incredible, it was a very emotional feeling. It was of someone that I loved." (7)

The work produced in one context presented in another encourages this kind of response and analysis. Needless to say, these pastels have caused considerable controversy, dealing with taboo subject matter so openly. Her next planned residence actually foundered before it began because of them, the vicar of a church school decreeing that the pastels could not stay in his school. Anne-Marie's initial reaction of "shock and disbelief that anybody could think like that" is quickly replaced by an acceptance "that I shouldn't be surprised at all". She wants to "dispel the myth and challenge peoples' response", clearing away the cobwebs, but it is frustrating and challenging to her that people are incapable of enjoying them for what they are; her work with young

people will hopefully lead to more informed attitudes when they become adults!

Anne-Marie works in natural cycles, devoting all her energies to the children's needs for a period and then channelling them into her own work. Dividing each week into half does not work for her, the 50/50 principle has to balance out over a longer time. Residencies evolve with a symbiotic relationship between her work and that of the children. A big part of her "just wants to do my own work. I have got a drive that needs channelling, that needs energy devoting to it". Yet if a school makes no educational demands on her that "doesn't fire me to produce my own work".

The Children's Library mural project

The Children's Library in Wigan was still under construction when Anne-Marie began the St James' Primary School residency with a brief to involve the children in murals for the library on a large expanse of grey wall, well above head height. Having previously enjoyed working in partnership with the head teacher at Hindley, she now struck up a particularly fruitful working relationship with the deputy head teacher at St James'. She describes him as "such an unconfident teacher, not with the children but in terms of his knowledge of the arts": he was in an Arts in Schools subject-specific development group and, as a primary practitioner, "he felt he was made vulnerable by the secondary teachers" there. Nevertheless, he was an influential teacher of dance and skilfully used this as a means to cross-curricular learning. It was through his Dance and Movement expertise that significant aspects of the work of this residency were generated - in particular, one huge group work.

"I remember the day we rolled out the big sheet of paper, the morning I drew the children and observed them, and through that they started to look at themselves...it was to do with trust, because they were having to make movements that relied on another person supporting them or catching them... Then when it came to drawing it was 30 people and a great big piece of paper, and allowing other people's statements and expression. For them to 'see' and to draw and explore their movements themselves on the paper - that was very moving."

Producing the library murals generated a wealth of creative writing and became a marvellous by-product of the main project. The aim was to involve every year in the school from reception to top junior. The chosen theme was the Four Seasons: each season was produced in season, studying its moods and atmospheres, flora and fauna - with the infants working on Autumn and Winter, lower juniors on Spring and the top juniors on Summer. As usual, Anne-Marie introduced the children to examples from art history, as Marina Vaizey noted when she visited the school to see the project.

"For the seasons' murals, farm animals have been brought into the school for the children to draw from; the children have visited farms, too, and been encouraged by some good hard looks at the work of such artists as Degas, Klimt, Gauguin and Monet, startling reproductions to find at primary school. It was fascinating to trace the influences the children had absorbed."

Anne-Marie's ability to bring works alive for children is one of her special gifts which she traces back to her sixth form college days when, "we were introduced to the work of Degas and Monet and Cézanne. There are so many ways in; it doesn't have to be done formally".

"When I had to do the murals and I was given a theme, it became clear to me that what I had done over the last couple of years in the Scheme was to actually make a painting have personal significance to a child. Every painting became a vital part of the way I expressed myself, and I suppose that is what I wanted to give to children."

She went to considerable lengths to make this happen, with the children dressing up and enacting paintings they were studying. For Pissarro's 'Apple Pickers', she brought in apples of her own, placed them in the trees in the school grounds to let the children experience the stretching sensations involved in reaching up to 'pick' them, whilst sketching each other. In her use of 'Les Parapluies' by Renoir, during work on the Winter panel, "I brought all my macs in and they had to stand on chairs so that the macs went all the way down to the floor, and they were holding umbrellas and were all hustled together."

"They became part of the colour, atmosphere and mood of the painting that they started off looking at, feeling part of it, part of the composition. They just became the characters and lived them and moved around on the picture and found new parts of it and new bits of colour, and showed parts of the picture to me that I hadn't seen before."

As with the Pissarro, the children entered into the spirit of Brueghel's 'Hay Making', carrying baskets on their heads. In relation to Millet's 'The Gleaners', one reception pupil, "having been posing bending down with a straw hat on and a sack of hay, went back to his teacher and said that he had been drawing blood-pressure". A six year-old boy, working on the Winter panel while Vivaldi's 'Four Seasons' was quietly playing in the background asked, "Why are my eyes wet, Anne-Marie?" It was doubtless the first time he had been moved to tears in such a way. "So that's another way into a painting where they're actually feeling it physically."

Two seven year-old girls produced their version of 'Olympia', the woman now asleep beneath a decorative blanket. One girl had been thinking about it while lying in bed the previous night, and thought it would be nice if she woke up to a cup of tea and cornflakes. These are now an amusing but decorative feature of the bottom left-hand corner. In addition,

"The children were doing a 'Happy Nevermore' where they'd understood the doom-laden significance of the raven and changed it into another bird, but a bird that didn't have the same significance, the same symbolism. The children there were interpreting something that they understood very clearly and making it into something that they wanted to say, changing the mood in the process - and doing it deliberately."

These are further examples of by-products of the main task of producing the murals. Now situated in the Children's Library, they are a 'must' for any visitor to Wigan. They comprise over 30' by 9' 6" of glowing children's imagery in which it certainly is "fascinating to trace the influences the children had absorbed" made possible through the ways in which Anne-Marie helps the children to relate their responses to situations to do with their own lives. When standing in front of these works it seems difficult to accept Brandon Taylor's arguments that primary children should be denied access to the works of others on the grounds that, "seriously wrong understanding is worse than no understanding at all". (8) What does "wrong" mean in this context? Surely these first joyous contacts with art - albeit through reproductions - are more likely to stimulate further interest and study than to fix "seriously wrong" ideas for evermore!

The intensity of her engagement with children

throughout that residency meant that Anne-Marie's own work barely ticked over, but on becoming the third artist to be resident at the Turnpike Gallery the balance was redressed. This post involved contact with school groups and the general public but gave her the necessary space to immerse herself in her own work for a year. A major theme running through the Turnpike work was her mother in her battle against the resurgence of cancer. Nevertheless, the resulting exhibition in the gallery was one of optimistic mood and "the feeling of celebrating women and their lives". To Anne-Marie, "the cancer was a

First year juniors working on the 'Spring' section of the Four Seasons mural.

A top junior working from a posed child in a deck chair in the 'Summer' section.

The Four Seasons mural on permanent display in the Wigan Children's Library.

The experience of stretching to pick apples in the Four Seasons mural 'Autumn' section - by reception pupils (left). Note the way the cat jumps out of the tree - by top infants (right).

This detail of the 'Spring' section shows a baby goat being bottle-fed.

Rich colour and boldness of design characterise this central area of the 'Summer' section.

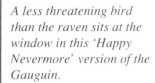

A less threatening bird than the raven sits at the window in this 'Happy Nevermore' version of the Gauguin.

metaphor, really, for a disappointing life of the woman and what she could achieve, and what it was possible for her to achieve".

A recurrent element in her work is the use of the written word. This originated through a friend - the deputy head teacher of Tyldesley County Primary - giving her a book, *My Mother's Body* by Marge Piercey, just before the residency. It was of poems about how a woman, in coping with her mother's death, had moved on to thoughts about her life. It was very meaningful to Anne-Marie at the time, and she began a collage by first writing out a poem and then covering it over.

"The poems would sort of absorb themselves, the lines in the poems, and absorb themselves into me and the layers, and then I would stop copying the poem out - it would come out as I conceived it, so it was always slightly different. They were more my mind pictures and covering them up then became wrong. They had a significance on the surface as well."

It was shortly after the Turnpike residency that she spent the month at Tyldesley on the 'My Body' project. She enjoyed the open yet demanding discussion and "all the sharing with the staff" which took place. Particularly satisfying, too, was the way the children made use of the layering processes in relation to a growing awareness of their own bodies - not unlike those used by Anne-Marie in her own collages which "were more reflective and probing, putting lots of things in and layering things in a way I couldn't do with a pastel drawing". Thomas, aged 10, gives expression to ideas about layering in this way in relation to his own body which are at a far remove from simply identifying organs as the teacher points to them on a drawn skeleton.

"When I was making my paper and putting pastel on tissue paper I felt I was putting myself together and when I was putting my pieces of paper in my book I felt I was putting the insides of me in my skin and it felt I was being made...My picture is about the softness and the beauty of our skin, and the warmth of my skin. The words in my picture make me feel safe about my skin. I drew clothes on my picture because it is about warmth and safeness of our skin." (9)

Compared with the majority of school residency schemes, a special feature in Wigan is that it harnesses the skills of young artists from within the same community. Anne-Marie had been educated in Wigan; many of her formative artistic experiences trace directly back to Wigan schools, as when she talks about making a painting "have a sort of personal significance to a child". It was through her own education that she first began to integrate gallery visiting, enjoyable in its own right, with her studio practice, and she is adept at helping young children to make similar connections. The Wigan Schools Loan Collection contains examples of her work from school and college days, enabling one to see how her talent has blossomed and developed. She is now one of the most experienced artists in the country at working in schools, and has proved herself to be an unusually sensitive communicator with young people of all ages.

Reproductions of Manet's 'Olympia' and Gauguin's 'Nevermore' led to these imaginative interpretations by junior pupils.

4 George Orwell and Children's Art for Public Places

"It's so lovely to see the children so absorbed in their work - they obviously enjoyed this experience."

"Extremely imaginative and a credit to all concerned."

"Very interesting, the children have obviously learnt a lot."

"A really talented young man who works well with the children." (1)

These are entries in the St Peter's Primary School, Bryn, visitors' book for the exhibition marking the culmination of Andy Shaw's residency. During that evening in April, 1989, there were many expressions of concern from parents that the impending National Curriculum might stop such educationally rich and worthwhile ventures in the future - rather ironic when one considers the wide-ranging nature of the learning experiences generated by the residency. These experiences are far more real and of longer-term significance than will be the case for young people who may find themselves in schools which focus narrowly on attainment targets, benchmark testing and national syllabuses.

Apparently the '3Rs' originally comprised Reading, Writing and 'Wroughting', acknowledging the fundamental part using one's hands and making has on learning. 'Wroughting' became 'rithmetic in Victorian times because of the need for clerks to add up ledgers in offices, and it has stuck ever since. Maybe the original version was the relevant one. Andy's residencies all illustrate the significance of wroughting, an all too frequently neglected aspect of many young people's education. Martin, aged ten, records,

"When I went to Andy I was lucky because he said we were going to be the first group to use his chisels and mallets. Before, the only good thing I could do with my hands was to pass a rugby ball properly. Andy taught me to chip in plaster and make papier-mâché. I liked the sculptor. I learned a lot. I want to be one when I grow up." (2)

The children's remarkable drawings filled the school hall covering every wall surface, and many sculptures displayed 'in the round' encouraging viewing from numerous angles. The eye-catching centrepiece was a raised up life-size donkey and Ian, also ten, offers an insight into the processes involved in its making - unusual ones in terms of most young people's experiences at this age.

"When I went to the sculptor I started by learning to weld because we had to help to weld the frame for the donkey. Then we used chicken wire to build up the donkey and then wrapped paper round it and we had to use what I called hamburgers. This was to build up the muscles on the donkey. Then we used papier-mâché and bits of paper...It all went hard and then we put on some fibreglass resin and in a few weeks we will be spraying it with spray guns." (3)

The donkey is not just any donkey, though. It is Benjamin from George Orwell's *Animal Farm* and the latest animal to be completed during Andy's various residencies over the last couple of years. Boxer, the shire horse, Napoleon, Snowball and Squeaker, the pigs, a magnificent cow, some sheep and a goat had all been built during earlier residencies, while Major, the white boar, and Bluebell, Jessie and Pincher, the border collie dogs, are the subjects of the next residency. All are life-size and constructed to resist the elements, because they are eventually to be located on the disused Platform No 7 on Wigan North Western Station, where they will form an unusual sculptural tableaux clearly visible to the numerous inter-city commuters from Scotland and the North to London.

The project arose out of a local amenity group plan to reclaim the platform by making it into an attractive feature through planting bushes and shrubs. They approached Drumcroon because a concrete slab along most of the platform's length defied all their design ingenuity. It was agreed that from then on it would be referred to as a 'plinth'. Having visited the site, Andy was keen that it should be a sculptural project and it was he who conceived the 'Animal Farm' theme as a way of linking the station to the nearby Wigan Pier complex, just a short walk away, with its many associations with George Orwell through his book, *The Road to Wigan Pier*.

"Animal Farm *was a book I'd read several times at school doing English Literature. It is a book I've enjoyed reading ever since, so it seemed a nice one as it had good connections with Wigan. There was Orwell and the animals and it had a political side. It was also good subject matter to use because we could bring English into it as well. All round it was an absolute winner." (4)*

Andy's dog sculptures and his use of them as a residency theme has already been mentioned, but the real prototypes for the 'Animal Farm' project were two life-size cows made during his second residency at Aspull Church School. With one frequently to be seen standing, the other lying, on the grass at the front of the school they rapidly became a popular local landmark. Andy says that the 'Animal Farm' concept

"...came about through having already taken on the problems of making life-size animals out of fibreglass and metal. Working with children of only 10 and 11, cows were twice life-size, four times the size of the children who were working on them...I went into it headstrong at Aspull, the results were fantastic...Since then we've tackled the problem in very similar ways every time even though we are dealing with different animals."

In each subsequent residency, the 'Animal Farm' sculpture has been the focus, with many smaller scale sculptural projects taking place around it involving various school groups. The pupils use a variety of techniques, processes and materials, building in clay, casting, working with plaster, using moulds, constructing directly with plaster mixed with straw, using papier-mâché and so on. The same well-tried procedures are followed in each residency, commencing with studies from life.

"We use the drawing process. We go out to see the animal first of all, which is very important. To date, we have seen every one of the animals...I could tell you many funny stories about going out into the fields and drawing and measuring different animals. Looking at them, doing very quick sketchy drawings, like the sketches of Phyllis Jones."

Andy Shaw's work in the foyer at Nicol Mere Primary School provides stimulus for discussion.

A corner of Andy Shaw's studio during his St Peter's, Bryn, school residency.

Andy makes extensive use of the framed sheet of drawings by Phyllis Jones which is in the Wigan Schools Loan Collection. It is made up of many sketches of horses and jockeys rapidly executed at the Haydock Park Racecourse,

While out in the fields, good use is also made of the tape-measure, an animal being measured for its height and length, including various limbs. The measurement from ear to back leg is always a significant one, even though the donkey used as the basis

 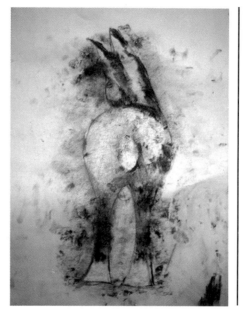

Working studies to aid their sculpture: many of the children's charcoal drawings from life are of extraordinary quality.

"I take them into schools and show the kids how she tackled the problem explaining that it wasn't really important to get a detailed bang-on portrait of whatever you were doing. It's just to get a feel of the movement and the shapes...I'm not bothered if those children come back with nothing at all. These drawings are working drawings which, in effect, we could drag through the mud or drop in the field. The looking is the most important part, and that's what I stress to the children, not the drawings. They're not precious, though they are precious in other ways because they are part of the process. We do refer to these drawings quite often."

for Benjamin kicked out wildly if its ears were accidently touched. For all Andy's insistence that the looking process predominates over the drawings, many of the children's studies, often in charcoal, are of stunning quality.

"The small drawings are scaled up when they come back, using the measurements they've taken. I think charcoal helps to give them a better feel of the shape, of the size and the problems of the movement which they're going to deal with."

These second-phase drawings are aids to assist in the translation back into the third-dimension, a process full of obvious appeal to the children.

Andy Shaw's drawing after first viewing the Wigan railway platform site.

"These are the living examples, if you like, probably more so - if I dare say it - than CDT (Craft, Design and Technology) would offer to them. So from these measurements we start to use the metal and we are talking about the materials at a down-to-earth level. We cut those to shape and we weld them together. Now if you can imagine children actually using electric welding equipment with gloves and goggles, it's a very exciting process. We go into it quite nervously, but once they've had one go at that welding machine, they all want to become welders all of a sudden. These children could quite competently tap-weld wrought iron gates. As well as art, they are

learning a technical side, though I tend not to look at them as separate."

As a precautionary measure, however, he welds over the top of what the children have done to ensure "that they're secure and don't blow away as the 10.20 Edinburgh to London speeds through Wigan". The armatures extend sufficiently below foot, hoof or paw level to ensure that they can be bedded securely into the concrete plinth.

As the children start building the body forms over the basic skeletal armature form, Andy hopes to have been able to "mention metal, plastic, chicken wire, vynamould, whatever, and for those industrial materials to be picked upon and taken back into a classroom".

"Then we go to the chicken wire, which is cut to shape and bent. Now I don't touch anything at this stage, I only demonstrate. The only time I interfere is when I say to the children, 'I think there is something going badly wrong!' I get them to stand back and I get the problems out of the children - make them talk about them, hint about little things, and let them sort out the problems themselves. Around that chicken wire we've got newspaper which helps to bulk the shape out, papier-mâché and resin over the top - but it's the shape which is the most important..."

The various processes enable the animals to be weatherproof but not too heavy, with the children able to control the forms and shapes of each animal to their satisfaction. In addition, a volume of other sculptural work arises out of each residency and this is valued, and even treasured, by the schools as one head teacher notes,

"The project he did with the infant children was also very, very good. We've still got it in school and it still arouses a lot of comment, even though it's 18 months now since it was done. It was a series of pictures in plaster and painted, which the children had cast. It was a day in the life of a child at the school. We get a lot of people having a look at it, people who come in - visitors and parents. It's a real asset." (5)

In making plaster and straw sculptures, one pupil observed that "a girl called Nicola Hicks worked in this way", and during the course of a residency Andy will carefully introduce the children not only to Hicks' works, but to those of Rodin, Moore, Marini, Caro, Flanagan, Frink and others, including such Drumcroon exhibitors as Ted Roocroft and Christine Merton. One of his dreams is that a whole school will one day seize upon what he is doing with the industrial implications of the processes being picked up on and the English implications similarly developed,

"...but I can guarantee that in every school I go into, at least one teacher will pick up on what I am doing, read the book Animal Farm, *actually talk about some of these materials, etc. I'd like to be able to pick up on that side myself, but obviously you're limited for time in a residency. Six months is quite a long span, but if you were to go into all this technical detail, you'd need a lot longer, but you could kill a lot of those problems off by making it a project through a whole school."*

At St Peter's, the one 'guaranteed' teacher used *Animal Farm* with her class of eight and nine year-olds, and it had a powerful impact on the children who preferred it to the stories they normally had. "I think I preferred *Animal Farm* to the ones we had before. I'd like to read it again." Their identification with the various characters ensured that they became emotionally involved and could freely discuss them months later.

"I liked Boxer. Well, when the teacher was reading it I had a picture in my head because I used to have a boxer dog, but when she said it was a horse I got a picture that it had a face like my boxer dog and it had a body and legs like a horse. When that bit came where he was took away to the knackers it made me very sad." (6)

Another child also experienced feelings to do with a former pet,

"At the end where he went to the knackers it made me feel as if I wanted Sam back - my old dog - because he died and I didn't know where to put myself until we got Jasper."

One girl's favourite character was Napoleon, "because he was a good character" even though he was bad.

"At the end, Napoleon started drinking ale and arguing like man. I think the animals were really cross with Napoleon...I'd have liked Boxer to have ruled because he always wanted to work harder than everybody else at making the windmill...They lied about Boxer when he was taken to the knackers. His last words were 'I shall work harder and long live Napoleon'."

41

They also knew the seven animal commandments and how they had been broken, because,

"...it said that no animal shall be dressed in clothes and no animal shall drink alcohol...and Napoleon was wearing clothes and drinking alcohol, and he slept in a bed...I'd really like to get it from the library because I really enjoyed that book."

When their animals eventually go on display on the station, there should be a good number of young people to whom they represent Orwell's animals, rather than just sculpted animals! Especially as the local media were attracted by the unusual and dramatic nature of the concept, "The farm animal now standing at platform...", followed by front page coverage,

"A rundown railway station is set to be transformed into an eye-catching scene from George Orwell's Animal Farm."
"Schoolchildren in Wigan are sculpting the four legged heroes from Orwell's novel in a bid to brighten up the town's North West station."
"In 18 months time, instead of ugly concrete, British Rail commuters will see a life-size menagerie...they will take up position on the presently disused loading platform at the station..."
"It should be quite an eye-catcher when it is finished," adds Andy. (7)

Boxer was made at Nicol Mere Primary School. The head teacher indicates that many people will take an above-average interest in the project once it is unveiled on Platform 7.

"It was very significant because it was such a positive influence on the work of the school. Literally everybody got involved one way or another, some more directly than others. It spread to parents, governors - everybody went to have a look at Boxer being made. There was an enthusiasm which I was particularly grateful for, because it brought a breath of fresh air into the school and it permeated every corner - even the caretakers and cleaners noticed. Everybody started looking at the art work in the school in general, I think, with a different sight...there wasn't a negative aspect." (8)

Andy had proved a natural catalyst in the school and "he was fantastic with the children". The head teacher adds,

"I don't know any group of people he can't get on with, the youngest children, the oldest children, the staff - everybody. Everybody likes Andy, everybody says, 'Yes, Andy Shaw!' with a smile. You never mention his name without a smile. Now, there aren't that many people in the world like that - something special. We all have these memories of Andy - some of us have bits of his work in our homes as well...he left his mark in such a way. Andy is quite a character and excellent for the job you want him to do..."

Andy is the classic example of the young Wiganer who readily identifies and communicates with young people to stunning effect. Nothing is too much trouble for him and he is always willing to enlighten visitors to his residencies by giving them an honest picture, faults included, of what he is about. Yet he turned down the offer of a place in the Artists in Wigan Schools Scheme when first approached!

"...I knew very little about Drumcroon and the way that it operated. I came down and saw what was happening with children walking round the gallery and everything, and I'll admit that did frighten me. I hid in the woodwork for about six months working in the shed at the bottom of the garden and turning out images which were no use to me or anybody else. I got no feedback and these ideas soon died out."

Having come into the Scheme with some hesitation and trepidation, how does Andy feel that it has benefited him some four years later? He was on the unemployed list and "would have taken anything - working on motorways - if it had come up at that particular time I would have taken it, and it wouldn't have happened what has happened today". He continues,

"I've made many contacts and many friends since working through Drumcroon and in the Artists in Wigan Schools project, and the most important thing to me is that I've developed as a person. I wouldn't have been the person that I am today. Confidence is one of the main things...The way I approach people and communicate with them is another. I look upon myself as a relatively shy and nervous type, but I've had more of a reputation of being more outgoing ever since I've been working in Wigan. It's not false, it's a true enthusiasm and energy which has been actually placed in me by the children. I suppose, more than anything else...I can tackle problems, I feel confident about going into things which I would never have even dreamed of."

The eventual shape and structure of a cow at the stage where chicken wire covers the welded armature.

Studies provide the basis for large-scale drawings prior to making the sculptures.

Fibreglass seemed a major technical problem to him while at college but now, he feels, there is "nothing too big or too small which I feel that I can't handle". On leaving college "I used to find things like talking and giving little bits of slide shows nerve-wracking and hated every second of it."

"But to be able to do all these things now and come away and think, 'I've enjoyed that!'...I think that's a massive notch up in your own book and for everybody else. Because I'm sure that as well as feeding myself, it does feed out in other people."

He finds his dealings with children particularly fulfilling, and he puts this down partly to his lack of preconception as to how he is going to work with them; he is not the type to "look through books and find out how to deal with them".

"I'll deal with that child as an individual and let that child talk back to me...I think you have got to be open-minded about an awful lot of things. Adults tend to think that we're the ones educating children and they can't teach us anything. But if you let that child develop as an individual and also in a group, and encourage that child to communicate as well, all of that comes back...it leads on quite naturally to how the children have influenced me as well."

He points to greater ease in the way he handles charcoal in his drawings and in his textural use of plaster as evidence of his debt to the children. He also sees the young people he works with as having their fingers clearly on the pulse,

"...when times are changing, I suppose children are the ultimate representations, really, because where fashion is, or to do with what's happening in television, or modern-wise, they're the ones who are more aware of it than we are. We're fine, thank you very much! We're settled into our lifestyles and we don't want to know anymore, we're quite comfortable. We've got to learn from those children what they'll be needing and what we can get out of them. I think there are some very important lessons to be learned there. I am open to the children's ideas and I get as much satisfaction out of the children's work as I do from my own...when I've walked into the studio in the morning, I find myself looking at the kids' sculpture nine times out of ten before looking at my own."

43

*Finishing touches to
Boxer the horse prior to
painting.*

Andy has learnt the art of listening to young people, and what he does with them constitutes a natural balance between drawing out while feeding in.

Naturally, British Rail have become interested in the project: they have provided sufficient funding to cover the cost of the materials and the eventual siting of the sculptures on the platform. There is no need to stress how children's motivations and involvements are affected by working on a project which is 'for real': their work is intended for display on a prime site within the community, as opposed to making 'art' at a prescribed time, some of it to enjoy a short life on the classroom wall but the remainder to be condemned to drawer or cupboard. The Artists in Wigan Schools Scheme has generated a whole body of work which bursts out of the all too familiar confines, an increasing amount actually being conceived and designed to be located on a long-term basis within the school itself or in the community. In the process, it frequently leads to cross-curricular work, as in the case of Andy's 'Animal Farm' project.

Of all these projects involving the transformation of school art into real life situations, the most spectacular should be 'Animal Farm', but the discerning viewer will doubtless detect evidence of rich learning experiences within it. A classroom teacher wrote to the Education Offices,

"I felt compelled to write to you to say a very big 'Thank You' for allowing Andrew Shaw the opportunity to teach at St Peter's School, Bryn. His enthusiasm and patience have been a lesson to us all. The work he has put in with our children is beyond words. My only regret is that he has had to move to another school. The children, not only my own, have loved every minute of his work." (9)

Not only did the school lose Andy, they also lost Joe the woodcarver. Joe's wife is the secretary at a previous school where Andy was in residence. Joe is now retired and enjoys carving. Not only did he receive support from Andy but he also responded to the interactive situation he found himself in on being invited to bring his work in to the school. So much so that he now moves from school to school with Andy, thoroughly enjoying himself - one further illustration of Andy's abilities to communicate with everybody, irrespective of age or ability.

Boxer the horse generated a great deal of interest at Drumcroon during the 1988 'Artists in Wigan Schools'

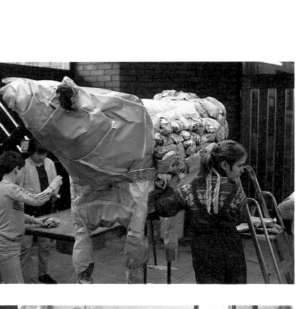

Un-named in Animal Farm, the children called the cow 'Fibre', seen here at the papier-mâché and 'paper hamburger' stage of construction.

Benjamin the donkey holding centre stage in the exhibition marking the culmination of Andy Shaw's St Peter's residency.

5

Special Needs and a Special Approach to Ceramics

"When I met Norma I knew that we were going to work well together because her attitudes were right. She didn't look at the child and say, 'This child has this big handicap'. She looked at the real child first, and saw what the child could do - not what the child couldn't do. That was very important...the children can sum up people so quickly. They're so shrewd and they knew that Norma was on their side and wanted to do the best for them, but in the right way. There was no false sympathy, which we don't need." (1)

Norma Tait's pots displayed amongst an impressive ceramic exhibition in the Leigh C of E High School Art and Design department during her residency

At her own request, Norma Tait began working in the special schools sector in January 1987. The head of Art at Mere Oaks (a school for the physically handicapped and the first special school in which Norma worked) spoke of her special attributes which fitted her for this work. The head of Art admits to getting "a bit prickly" about those who come into the special school sector "overloaded with sympathy" and wanting "to work out their own feelings...all on the sympathy side". By comparison Norma's con- cerns were always for the pupils as individuals and her approaches positive, starting from their needs. Another advantage was that

"Her work was so totally honest and real to the children. There's a simplicity in her work, but not because it's crude or simple, because it's an easy way of doing it. It's simple because it's honest and there is a real truth there. Children immediately latch onto that truth."

Norma is a ceramicist whose pots 'give eloquent expression to her love of simple shapes and hatred of anything over-elaborate or ostentatious', but she does admit to sometimes "getting carried away with the top". What she seeks in her work, above all other things, is a 'powerful simplicity'. In her Mere Oaks residency she struck up a working partnership with the head of Art which came close to the ideals of partnership which the Artists in Wigan Schools Scheme was founded upon. For example, the head of Art explains,

"I would say something and she would say something, and things would grow from our togetherness. We bounced off each other. Going our own ways, OK, fine. But together we had more power. We could get down to the nitty-gritty of things...and, also, it's a process. There was Norma, there was myself and there were the children, and we were all bouncing things off each other. It was not somebody saying, 'This is right and this is what we are all going to do'. We changed things as we went along...We were enthusiastic, but it was not a phoney enthusiasm. It was because it was exciting and it was fun...You get low expectations from people because they see the handicap first and not the child. This is what Norma and I don't do because we get excited and say, 'Look at this!' and gather up the other person with you - and then you've got somebody else giving you ideas."

In a genuine partnership, there is giving, receiving and sharing in equal measure, and this was certainly the case here, for Norma also indicates the extent to which she, too, benefited from this experience,

"I think I blossomed there. Right from the minute I walked into her Art room and looked round, it was obvious that she liked what I liked, and that helped...Listening to her talking to the children, I admired how she dealt with them and I admired how she taught her Art. When we were talking about something we were doing with the children, we always knew what each other meant and could always add something or suggest something. It's just rapport, isn't it?...And another thing, we both had projects that we were keeping for the time when we had the energy and opportunity to do them, and we found that we could get these projects implemented between us. On your own you think, 'I wonder if I could manage this!' We'd talk about it and then we'd say, 'Yes, of course - great. We'll do it! We will do it'. Working together we had the confidence and the energy to do it."
(2)

Through this close partnership, aided by Wigan's involvement in the Arts in Schools Project, both have subsequently benefited large numbers of pupils across the special needs spectrum in a variety of schools. Norma sees herself as having blossomed at Mere Oaks, although she had already spent a year

An ancestor pot made by primary pupils who worked in the Leigh C of E Art and Design department as part of Norma Tait's residency.

Detail of the figures on the ancestor pot representing the peoples of the world.

working in Wigan high schools having been one of the first two artists appointed to the Scheme from outside Wigan. An approach had been made to the 3-D Department at Manchester Polytechnic because there was a need to appoint a ceramicist. A lecturer approached Norma who 'knew something good was happening in Wigan' and came for a meeting at St Andrew's and "it just seemed so exciting what was happening, it was the Fantasy Village" and she remembers "catching the infectious attitude. There just seemed to be some sort of spark that was around", and she had no hesitation in accepting a place on the Scheme.

With hindsight she is able to identify a sequence of experiences which strengthened her conviction

"...that 'special needs' are lumped together nearly always, as if there were one universal 'special need'. And there isn't. Each person is special. I think everybody has got special needs - all of us..."

In her first residency she confesses that she did feel quite alone. "I did have the support of Drumcroon, but within the school I felt alone." Nevertheless, she was able to establish a special rapport with, on the surface, the most unlikely and seemingly unpromising group of pupils.

"...I got a lot of the kids who had got absolutely nothing out of school. They didn't do any exams and they were leaving at Easter. They spent most of their time in the pottery and they did some really good work. In fact, they entered them for the CSE exam, so they got a qualification out of the school."

She recalls that, in the end, other staff came over to the ceramics studio, "out of curiosity to see what they had done that was so good that they could take an exam", and,

"I think that's when it started, wanting to work with special needs, because I enjoyed their company. And I always found that they always worked well, they were less inhibited in some of the things that they would try."

The book *Artists-in-Schools: Analysis and Criticism* makes the criticism that "more than 80% of artists and poets had little or no contact with problem students", but this is not the case in Wigan, and Norma in particular reached many to whom the conventional system was unable to offer anything.

She established an extraordinary working relationship with one pupil, Darren,

"He wasn't badly behaved at school, he just didn't work as hard as he could have done because I don't think he was very interested in the things they were doing. He used to say, 'Oh, it's dead boring, drawing shells!'...He worked very well in pottery, he was very good."

Darren describes himself as, 'rebelling against Art because it didn't relate to life,' and when Norma began her residency he was told to go to her in Art lessons. Within a couple of weeks he had mastered basic coiling techniques and a large pot, the first of an impressive series, was well underway. He became so engrossed that he worked out his designs at home, establishing a momentum that ensured his next idea was clear in his mind before the work in hand was completed, so as to avoid fallow or unfruitful periods in the ceramics studio.

Darren's work was afforded a prominent place alongside Norma's in the Turnpike Gallery's 'Surface to Surface' exhibition where it delighted many visitors, and Darren and his family were proud attenders at the preview. Norma worked in residence at the gallery during the exhibition, this added to her conviction that her destiny was in special schools,

"...working on the workshops at the Turnpike with the special needs groups of adults that came in. Some were mental handicaps and I found them interesting. Just the way that one man came up to me and said things like, 'Look at me. There's not a mark on me. You wouldn't think I'd been killed in 1942'. Things like that made me stop and think. It was quite bizarre in a way. It made me interested in them. I wanted to find out and to work with people with different minds - I thought I got something from that. I can't really explain what it is."

Another formative experience was working on a rota with other artists for an evening a week at the Youth Treatment Centre for young offenders.

"They had to go there in the evenings. That was a last chance. If they got into any more trouble with the police they would be locked up. Now that was pretty early on and I enjoyed their company. I enjoyed the sharp edge to them. There was a certain electricity in the air, it was potentially explosive and it could all go wrong...They are very exciting to be with especially the speed of their

Norma Tait assisting a Mere Oaks pupil to experience the tactile qualities of pots and natural forms in the display.

repartee! I find different people very interesting - the people on the edges."

As a consequence of those various experiences, Norma asked if she could officially work in the special needs sector. She moved to Mere Oaks in January 1987, and all her subsequent residencies have been in Wigan special schools. It was a broadening experience, also, because the teacher's approach was to

"...work individually and she would ask a lot from them. Not a pat on the head - 'That's nice. Good for trying!' Rather, 'You haven't tried enough and can't you see this?'"

But in a constructive way and in a climate which eschewed low expectations,

"And not just in the visual arts. She would take them to the theatre and make them discuss it afterwards and ask opinions. You weren't allowed to say you didn't like it, you had to say why. Not only that - the newspapers. They'd discuss topics in the newspapers at registration in the morning...It was almost a whole education in the Art room, really."

In addition, some of the children's poems written in that room are quite exceptional.

Norma's displays of Schools Loan Ceramics and reproductions of material she had collected on gallery and museum visits were impressive from the outset, but they took on new dimensions at Mere Oaks.

"That was because of the way the Art teacher introduced me to the children. She asked questions like, 'What would you display with these pots?' A lot of the things I'd got but hadn't unpacked - bits of dried grasses, rusty metal, seed pods, even feathers. They went round their Art room and got them and put them there. I learnt from her about displaying other materials with the pots. Up till then, mine were just things I put on the wall, really, and maybe an odd collection of stones."

When Norma visits the Art teacher's home, it is always the occasion for the collection of some 16 or so of her pots housed there to be rearranged and seen afresh, as the teacher explains,

"When Norma comes to my house it is always important that she sees where they are and how they are displayed and what they are displayed with, because I put other objects with the pots."

At Mere Oaks they constructed displays in which Norma's pots were skilfully juxtaposed with a variety of manufactured and natural objects. Not precious

A display featuring Norma Tait's pots at Mere Oaks Special School arranged by pupils, teacher and artist working together.

displays, though, for these were tactile, meant to be explored physically as well as visually, and incorporating the children's work. According to the Art teacher,

"You can have wonderful displays that mean absolutely nothing, but when you have got a display it's all about doing honour to the kids, to the kids' work and they're part of it and the kids have the say in how they're going to do the display. It's all part of the process."

Such displays were also particularly appropriate to Norma's work, with their 'earthy' qualities, absence of glazes and experimental firing methods. For, after a first firing in the kiln,

"I try to decide what sort of finish would suit the pot. If I want it really blackened I usually put it in sawdust and try and contain the smoke which reduces the oxygen and the pots go dark, but if I want a softer colour I usually use peat or leaves to burn it in. Sometimes I have grasses or flowers round them, and that sort of marks off certain areas. You can get very delicate patterns showing through, like veins on clover. You couldn't arrange a precise design, at best it's a bit haphazard. You can control it to a certain extent but not precisely and I wouldn't want it to be too precise because I like co-operating with the fire...I like bonfires."

Her work had developed almost imperceptibly since leaving college, but during the Mere Oaks residency an important development took place which Norma could locate exactly. She started embellishing her pots by adding objects like animals, lizards and birds to the rims. Though she had been considering doing this for some time, she now finds it hard to believe that she hesitated for so long.

"It seems such a simple step but it was very difficult to take...I had finished a pot but it didn't look quite finished and I didn't know what to put on the top of it. I was just twisting clay into shapes pushing them around the rim. I twisted it into the shape of a bird and I made a few more and just sat them round the top and I was thinking, 'Does it look silly?'"

Just at that moment the Art teacher walked past and commented, "Oh, I like that!" and confirmation from somebody whose opinion Norma respected was enough. "That was it, the step was taken." Such

a distinctive motif as the pelican on a pot made at Tanfield Special School had obvious appeal to young people. It came from a midsummer holiday experience when she saw a pelican.

"It was sitting, a beautiful shape. It was folded back on itself, it was like a blob and its head wound right to the back of its body and its beak came back again to the front. I was leaning over to take a photograph of it. All of a sudden it changed shape and ran at me complaining - quite rightly, really. It was really cross and it had its beak open, and it was just this beak chasing me that stayed with me, and that appeared on a pot based around this picture in my mind."

However, the shape came out of a 'culmination of a few things' because,

"I had the scythe as well, this rusty scythe that I'd dragged in from the grounds just because I liked the colours and the way the wood had gone black with age. I had that around, and it was the beak - the memory of the pelican - and a postcard I'd bought of a woodcarving of a bird with a really big beak...they just came together in a piece of clay one day when I was looking for a shape to finish a pot."

Michael was one pupil who responded to Norma's work at Mere Oaks. He had painted with the Art teacher for some time, using a brush screwed into a canoeing helmet and operating a computer with his right foot to work out some of his graphic designs. The Art teacher felt that

"He'd come through a certain process with the painting and he could accept Norma's work, whereas a lot of kids want things glazed and coloured and highly polished, and sort of manufactured, because that is what they've looked at all their lives. But he could see there was an honesty, a truth and a simplicity that didn't mean it was naive, he could see that...he was ready for Norma, he was, 'Right, let me try, let me have a go at this'. OK he could see that because the edges were raw, there was a certain beauty about that. Also, he could say, 'that goes with corn husks, or with pine cones'. He could see that connection with them as well, what was right with them."

Michael's ceramics achievements were extraordinary. He was into his CSE exam when Norma started there and she kept an eye on him when the Art teacher went off sick before he had finished. Norma takes up the story.

"Then when he had finished, he used to come and watch me working. I didn't think he could do anything in pottery because he can't use either hand and he can only control one foot. He put his foot on the table and rolled a piece of clay one day. I thought, 'Well, if he can do that he can make pottery'. So between us we devised ways that he could do it - he could roll a rolling pin, so he rolled a slab of clay. We went round the room until he found a shape he wanted and I just lifted the slab of clay over the shape and left him to do what he wanted with the edges. He folded them back, trimmed them with his toes, back-heeled it into position and made all the decisions. He couldn't do the things like joining two pieces together, but he made it clear what he wanted to be joined and where. So he showed me that he could do it, and in doing so I now believe everybody can do something. I see it as my job to find the way for them to do it. He liked a particular shape, so I made him a plaster shape that he could use."

He used his helmet brush to apply the glazes, and his ceramic skills alongside those developed in painting made Michael a very fulfilled young person. Unfortunately there was a great deal of frustration in store for him. He went to a college some distance from Wigan and when the warden of the hall of residence saw Michael's ceramics he wanted him to continue, leading to Norma teaching him at a night class she still runs. So far so good, but,

"He went to the college, to this special needs Art class where they were drawing round templates and, of course, he was written off because he can't draw round templates because he can't hold a pencil. He was bored and he was considered to be a bit of a trouble-maker. Michael was able to communicate with those who had got to know him but another problem at college was that they weren't understanding him."

Michael found himself having to paint butterflies out of his imagination, and this really upset him. Messages that he had Grade 1 CSE and ought to be doing something more demanding and that he could use a computer were of no avail. Somebody who taught A-level did go to see him and a show was made of taking him to see where it was taught to emphasise that it was upstairs and inaccessible to him. It was stated that he could not draw or meet written demands required by A-level.

"I said, 'Well, he can draw on the computer'. They said they didn't think that would be acceptable so I suggested they contacted the examining board and asked them...I passed the information on that he could do an AEB exam without a written paper, and I passed it on not only to the A-level teacher but also to the people in charge of the special needs for them to sort out."

The response to the work Norma took in was that, "Well, perhaps it did look good in a special school!" And Michael said that the A-level teacher did not even bother to look at it.

"I took it back to Mere Oaks and Michael lost interest. It wasn't going to happen, he wasn't going to be able to do his A-level."

He was very hurt and upset at the time, but he is now doing well in his English and Maths and a Computer Studies teacher has discovered his ability to play computer chess and his other skills and says that a lot of time could have been saved if people knew what Michael could do to start with. Michael seems quite happy at the moment.

Claire was another pupil whose noteworthy ceramics achievements arose out of Norma's conviction that everybody has the capability to do something so long as they are assisted to find the means,

"She could squeeze but not let go, so it was very difficult for her to coil build because if she squeezed the coils together she ripped them, she went right through. So I found her a ridge tile and a drainage tile (they are circular), and I found her things to press against, porous things. She could get a lump of clay and bash it down and she'd aim it. She'd take a long time getting her aim right and then she'd just knock that down...it was a bit like dry stone-walling."

Norma continued,

"...it's just a matter of finding things that would help them produce something that was theirs. It had to be theirs. It was no good if you did it for them because they hadn't achieved it...It wouldn't mean anything to them."

Susan was a particularly rewarding pupil in Norma's terms. She had autistic tendencies and responded

Norma Tait explaining her use of inlay techniques to two Mere Oaks pupils.

Michael using his helmet brush to glaze a bowl.

A Mere Oaks pupil deriving obvious pleasure from the small pot of Norma Tait's which she is affectionately holding.

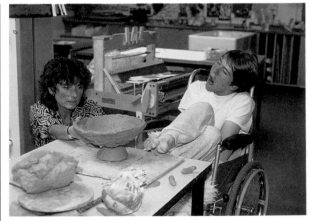

positively to Norma. "She let me see things. I felt privileged...I got a glimpse into her world." Susan went from saying,

"'I hate you!' and not looking at me, to coming up and giving me a kiss and saying, 'I didn't miss you this weekend'. At first she was only like that with me, but then she got a bit more confident herself and she goes to the Tech now...she went for one day a week then she asked if she could go there all the time, and she's coping. But the bits of her world I saw were governed by fear: the way she walked down a corridor, she was trying to get as close to the wall as she could and wouldn't look at anybody."

Red Nose Day worried Susan for weeks in advance and, "the thing is, I can identify with some of it; it's like me exaggerated. One day she said to me 'I hate fun'. I knew what she meant because it wasn't 'fun' that Red Nose Day, it was frenetic, it was awful. Susan felt that she could not cope with it - but she got through it!"

One Schools Loan item beloved by Norma and which she has made extensive use of is the 'Zombie Woof' mask by David Kemp, made from 'found' materials. Susan constructed a mask of her own which was exhibited in the Drumcroon 'Connections' exhibition. Susan had the surprising experience of visiting the Centre with a group from the

Michael's bowl after being through the bonfire smoking process which Norma Tait frequently favours in her work.

Norma Tait and Michael with one of his bowls at Mere Oaks.

Technical College and being confronted by her own work about which she had written, laughing the whole while,

*"Did you ever see
A straw rustle brush moustache
A pinch rubber screw nut nose
Hilarious spoke on spoke
Twang boy-oyong."*

Another feature of the 'Connections' exhibition was a striking set of ridge tiles made by the Mere Oaks pupils. Most of the work derives from a visit, usually to a museum, but these came from a Chinese ridge tile in the Burrell Collection seen in a book,

"Everybody decided to do the ridge tiles. They liked the idea of something that was frightening and that could protect them from evil spirits, which was what the Chinese ones were intended to do. They were at either end of the ridge on a roof to frighten away evil spirits."

The pupils discussed images which might create fear and thought about spikey forms. The resulting ridge tiles were individual and distinctive, even though there was a unifying theme and format.

"We talked a long time - is a round shape frightening? Is a spikey shape? How could you portray something frightening? You could make it figurative with a weapon. You could bare teeth. You could just have a frightening, spikey shape. We looked at how people had done this in other times. We looked through all the museum books and they said, 'that must have been used to frighten somebody!' We looked at Maori carvings that stand outside houses to frighten the enemies away. Canoe heads and so on. So we put quite a lot into it to get to things that were frightening."

Norma has a great love of old things, not only pottery,

"I'm still working out what it is about ancient things and ancient pottery. I think it's the lack of refinement. It's still clay. It's getting a bit modern for me if it's got glaze on. It's before glazes when clay was still clay and not covered up. It's the spirit they were made in, somehow. It seems as though this lack of refinement is an honesty. I think honesty is something else I particularly like about people with special needs. They are very honest, whether the special problem is bad behaviour, physical disability or learning disability. It's all very honest - even the bad behaviour is honest. I think this is all tied up with glazes, somehow! I'm not sure what it is!"

Her next residency was at Rosehill Special School where she had to contend with one manifestation of the pupils' behavioural problems which caused them to destroy what they were making, born out of a fear, she felt, that it might not turn out right, allied to peer pressures about not complying.

"They dealt with it by working really hard when they were with me and then being twice as naughty in other lessons. They tried that for a start. They behaved when they were working on what they wanted, then they made up for it around school. But that regulated itself, as did the wanting to destroy it before it was finished. Once they had a bit of security about success, they were a lot easier to deal with."

Allied to her love of ancient things relating to the earth, Norma also makes use of ancient fables and creation myths, such as,

"How the hare got its split lip and how the tortoise got its cracks, because they like to hear stories, they responded well to that. They are fairly simple, but we can make them simple or complicated, but the children remember the principal points and it meant something to them to be making a pot of a story."

This was certainly the case in a school where the children had severe learning problems, where Norma still went into some depth, because "otherwise you are fiddling about on the surface", and "you have to look at traditions for it to mean something". Much of the resulting work is of a group nature, with the children's figures all coming together on one large celebratory pot.

"With some of the younger children, aesthetics go by the board sometimes, because if you were making the decisions there would be three less people or objects on the pot, but you can't leave three people's out. Theirs have to go on, they have to be made room for. We do look and say, 'They don't all have to be packed together'. Considerations are given to shapes, proportions, forms - it's a combination."

A classic example of this process allied to ancient forms and stories arose out of a primary residence during Norma's first year in the Scheme. The school was involved in the national 'My Body' project which, though science-led, had taken on many new dimensions through art initiatives in Wigan. One of Norma's predilections is for Nigerian Ancestor pots.

"They had been looking at families and their relationships with other people, and that gave me the idea of showing them ancestor pots, pots with people on, family. I told them that it's part of the belief that when you die if one person remembers you, you are immortal. So a way of ensuring your

immortality is to make a pot with your ancestors on and you, so that if you are there people will look at it and are bound to remember you - so you are guaranteed your immortality. So they made their own pot to ensure their immortality. It doesn't look like an African pot, because it's brightly coloured and some have got football shirts on, but it's theirs."

Norma has exhibited quite widely, but has ambivalent feelings about the gallery world with its dependence on fashion and the power to make or break artists. However, there were no reservations about participating in Drumcroon's 'Connections' and 'In the Round' exhibitions.

"'In the Round' was so exciting, the first exhibition apart from putting a degree show together and this was somehow much more professional, more important in a way, and it showed more sides of me, I suppose, because it included children's work as well...I don't think I was aware until then how much my work had changed. I wasn't really aware of the big step I'd taken since leaving college...I'd gained a lot of confidence, really."

This was one year out of college, with 'Connections' following two years later and Norma confident enough "to create the environment that I wanted", in keeping with the concept of the exhibitions in which two ceramicists and two textiles artists from the Scheme were invited to display their work alongside that of their pupils. But they were also asked to look back to formative influences and interests which had affected their development, the whole came together within an appropriate setting.

"I had to convince people that I really wanted bricks, pieces of rusty metal, old step ladders. They were important, I wanted those there and I could see the worry on people's faces that it might look like a builder's yard, but by then I'd got the confidence to hold out...we managed to borrow things and bring in junk, things that go back into the earth. So that showed my influences, rather than people."

In the event, the effect was stunning and key items were the large Nigerian batik in indigo dyes and two decorative Indian window shutters, not only borrowed from the Wigan Schools Loan Collection but actually chosen for it by Norma, as she had been given the brief to make some purchases.

"That was wonderful being able to do that. That gave me a lot of satisfaction because I can use the Nigerian batik, I've got it with me now...I bought things which were a compromise between what I liked and what had mileage in them for the children - pattern and repetition, the freshness of design of some of these stylised animals and plants in the fabrics."

She believes that she is "an artist who needs other people and I like being with children, young or older", and so working in schools suits her temperament. She also believes that the 50/50 principle suits her and has positively benefited her work,

"...because I can't deliberate for too long, which I'm inclined to do...you can't just keep putting something away and getting it out, because they want to know what is happening to it. 'Haven't you finished that one you were doing yesterday? What's happened to it? Let's have a look.' So they keep the pressure on me and I keep the pressure on them."

Her work also takes on some of its characteristics and features from the atmosphere in which she is working. In one school the pupils' emotional disturbances found direct manifestation in Norma's work,

"When I was there it influenced me in the creatures I made on my work. I made some very tortured animals when I first went there, listening to all the howls and the arguments going on around school - dogs with arched backs, snarling teeth, and worm-like creatures curled up on themselves, protecting themselves."

Norma feels a growing realisation that working in this kind of interactive situation is right for her. Though she made the conscious decision to come into the Scheme, she sees it as "a happy accident", and she believes that if she had worked on her own at home it would have eventually become apparent to her that she had to do something similar to what she is doing now, probably in a youth centre. "I would have been nowhere near where I am now, because Wigan is just geared to everything I want to do. It would have been much harder to go it alone somewhere, but I would have tried it."

But let us conclude by returning to the Art teacher of Mere Oaks Special School. Through the Arts in Schools Project, as has already been indicated, she spends one day a week using her skills in the Authority's other special schools, based on which school

Norma is in at any given time, meaning that a special partnership continues to evolve. The teacher has gained immeasurably from this partnership.

"Norma opened up so many things for me. She took me places I hadn't thought of going before. I was more open to Drumcroon. I admit in my own mind, though I had been before, she made me see what I could do with Drumcroon. I suddenly realised what a wonderful richness there was there...It's there for us, and it's the best! You're not dealing with the mediocre or the average...I'm buying books that I wouldn't have looked at before: The Art of Africa, The Jewellery of Africa, *and looking at Indian art. I always bought rugs and artefacts, but I never really used them in the proper way and Norma showed me that I could...It's just opened up a different way, a very important way, of looking at things, especially for the children that we are dealing with. I'm certainly better as an Art teacher for having met her. I'd been teaching for a long time and you need that input, you need that support. It was so good. It recharged my batteries and gave me that excitement again."*

Norma says that if she was working alone she would probably often have the studio walls clean and bare, but through her brief to create an environment she has now introduced countless pupils to African, Maori, Aboriginal, Chinese and Indian art etc. She stresses that she had never set out "to do multiculturalism", but nevertheless offers an interesting model through her application of the 'Ripple Model'.

An Aboriginal Schools Loan display in the 'Drumcroon: the First Ten Years' exhibition. Some works were purchased in Australia from the money raised by raffling the pot donated by Norma Tait, displayed on the box to the right.

Norma Tait with pupils of Tanfield Special School sitting with pride in front of the 'Rousseau' project to which all the children in the school contributed.

Norma Tait and pupils' work is displayed at Drumcroon within the rich multicultural environment she created for the exhibition 'Connections'.

6

'On Being a Black Artist in Britain'

"Although I think it is important that children have access to the art and design of other traditions...I feel very strongly that the missing link is the contemporary black artist. I believe it is these people who can help us with our difficulties in terms of criteria for selection of Art objects as well as making an important contribution to the totality of mainstream Arts activity...I feel that a reliance on a scholarly, ethnographic approach is to present a picture which distorts the truth and does a disservice to British people of minority ethnic group origins." (1)

These words were written in a letter to me dated 28th January 1987 by a member of the Multicultural Education Resources Centre in Bedfordshire. The letter arose out of our conversations about the contrasting pictures in two Authorities, one a shire county with a high Afro-Caribbean and Asian population and the other, Wigan, where they constitute only about 1% of the population. As in most such communities, a common response amongst teachers is that it is not an issue - there is only one black pupil in their school. Wigan's involvement in the Arts in Schools Project has done much to counter this viewpoint and to enable teachers to think through the Seven Wigan Principles of which two read as follows:

(Above right) 'Education must take place within an international context...': this display celebrated and reinforced the residency of Edith Proctor, an African dancer, at Hawkley Hall High School.

The impact was complemented by a richness and intricacy of detail inviting closer scrutiny of particular works.

"2. Education must take place within an international context as opposed to the national context within which it has operated to date.

5. Education must take cognisance of the rights of the individual and encourage mutual respect between individuals and between ethnic and cultural groups." (2)

Kevin Johnson joined the Artists in Wigan Schools Scheme in January 1989. It was as long ago as June 1987 that he was offered a place in the Scheme on the basis of the impact which his work made on me in the foyer of Bretton Hall College where he obtained a BA Honours degree. A place was held open for him on the Scheme while he did the PGCE year at the same College, and was deferred for another term while he undertook a sculpture commission in Manchester, at which stage he also became a member of the Black Artists Alliance.

On joining the Scheme Kevin rapidly demonstrated how essential the presence of the black artist is. Great efforts had been made to broaden the range of the Wigan Schools Loan Collection which, along with virtually all other such collections, had initially evolved in a Eurocentric manner. Drumcroon consciously constructs its exhibition programme to take account of race, gender and special needs and the range, breadth and variety of the visual arts. Also, as has been seen, some of the artists skilful exploitation of the 'Ripple Model' introduced pupils to non-European Art. Many teachers had made great strides in thinking through their involvement in the Arts in Schools Project which had race as one of its major concerns. All these conscientious and sincere efforts suddenly seemed insignificant when Kevin spoke 'On Being a Black Artist in Britain' at a residential Art and Design Conference for Wigan teachers at Grange-over-Sands on 19th February 1989. Following are three responses to his talk:

"'On Being a Black Artist in Britain' brought forth many complex reactions as he was articulate, funny, honest and moving. Behind his benign exterior some very disturbing items emerged which will stay with us and influence our teaching long after the Conference has faded."

"...a very moving presentation reminding us all of the silent messages conveyed by our choice of subject matter and reference material."

"Excellent, moving, thought-provoking and challenging. Kevin must be an asset to the Scheme." (3)

In the Conference Pack accompanying Kevin's session there was a paper entitled, 'Anti-racism and Multiculturalism in the Visual Arts'. It made use of a Bedfordshire policy statement, setting it in relation to the Wigan Principles,

"Education should prepare people for life in the wider community and help them to develop attitudes and ways of behaving which are appropriate to living in a society which wishes to eradicate racial prejudice and the social scars it produces. All pupils and students (whether belonging to majority or minority groups) need to have their awareness heightened of the multicultural society within which they live. The aims for the Education Service in a multicultural society are thus identified as:-

(i)   to meet the specific educational needs of all groups having regard to their ethnic or cultural backgrounds;

(ii)   to develop an understanding of and a positive response to the multicultural society (in the region);

(iii)   to combat racism and any discriminatory practices to which it gives rise." (4)

After the weekend, one primary teacher spoke of the value of the Pack, and went on to say,

"...I am in the midst of compiling a Creative Arts Policy for the School. Many of the points made were of particular validity - Anti-racism and Multiculturalism in the Visual Arts - to encourage an awareness and respect between Ethnic and Cultural groups - to develop a positive response to the Multicultural Society combating racism..." (5)

It is important to dwell upon policies because, even though they do not necessarily bring about change, without them good intentions can lack focus and even prove counter-productive.

At Grange-over-Sands Kevin captivated 70 teachers by relating his powerful work to his life's experiences. The magnitude of the issues involved came bitingly alive; anti-racism and multiculturalism raise special issues in predominantly white communities, as Kevin's own early experiences emphasise.

"...we moved to a middle class area of Nottingham which is mainly white. There were only five of us in the entire school and there were very few of us in the neighbourhood anyway. So you always felt inferior - everyone in the top group was always white, all the teachers were white, all the doctors were white, everywhere you went they were always white. But if you wanted to see who was doing the bins, they were probably black. The nurses at the hospital were black. You rarely saw any positive roles. My mother was a nurse, my father is a welder, therefore living up to the stereotype - no disrespect to them, but that was how it was. So I actually felt negative about being black..." (6)

The last thing he wanted to do was to give expression to his being black in his work,

"When I did self-portraits they were always white. I'd have, like, black features but I would never dream of colouring my face in because it just didn't look aesthetically right, because black was the negative...I don't think I drew a black person until I was at college..."

His cousins, brought up in a black area of London, excelled in their education and could not accept Kevin nor he them, for they saw him as a black person who was white and to him they were too black to identify with. Going to college at 16 was, therefore, quite traumatic.

"...my first day when I walked in, there were so many black people I just couldn't handle it, I really couldn't handle it at all. I wouldn't sit with them. I walked in the canteen and saw them all there and just walked straight out again and sat in the ceramics room with all the other white people. I went home and my mum says, 'How was college, Kevin?' And I said, 'It was good but...there are too many black people there'. And she said, 'But you are black, Kevin. You are black!' I said, 'That's not the point. There are just too many of them there!'"

Eventually he began to make friends, and found that their cultures were the same and there was nothing negative about it. A history lecturer led him to look at black history with its positive achievements, but Kevin began to feel angry at having felt so negative for so long because of this withdrawal of information, compounded by a hospital stay following being beaten up by a National Front Group. He embraced Rastafarianism as a symbol of being black, never lost an opportunity to challenge white people and went through a rebellious and aggressive phase, at the same time wanting to do something more positive.

"One day my mother sat me down and said, 'You're so bitter against white people but you're not doing anything for the cause. You're actually reinforcing the stereotypes by doing what you've been doing...The only way if you want to beat the system is to get in the system and carry on like that you're not going to do it'. What she said made sense...and then I got a place at Bretton Hall."

Having got there, he still did the wrong thing. He failed to realise his own identity and instead found African images from library books as if to prove himself as a black person he had to say, "All my work has got to be African". One day a lecturer challenged him and said, "You're not African, you're Black British and you've got to face it". Kevin felt frustrated and unfulfilled until a visiting artist, Hugh O'Donahue, told him to forget about his degree and to simply express himself by doing what he wanted to do.

Kevin produced his first ceramic head and was really pleased with it and went on to produce others, in the process establishing the distinctive working methods which characterise his work to this day and have powerfully affected the pupils who have come into contact with him in Wigan at St John Fisher High School. A visiting teacher reporting on his residency wrote,

"Kevin had been working in the school for just a term when I visited. He had set up his studio between the two Art rooms and had clearly made quite an impact on the pupils of the school. All around the studio are sculptured busts produced larger than life and in a strong, powerful style...The underlying theme to his work is based on being black in Britain. He explained that the pupils had reacted well to his work and that many of them had produced sculptures themselves trying the fast expressive style...The main influence however was surely that Art can be used to

portray a message and Kevin had certainly done that provoking interest in the wider issues of racism and a multicultural society...The head of Art explained that she had very much welcomed the stimulus provided by the artist-in-residence and valued the contribution he had made." (7)

Kevin adopted approaches at Bretton which enabled him to get rid of all his feelings of anger at that time. He no longer had need to delve into African Art books, nor even to make preparatory drawings. He relied on his own personal experiences and believes that these are by no means exhausted yet.

"What I would do, I would just lock myself away from everything, which is very easy to do at Bretton because you can just sit in the sculpture park. I would think about things that had happened to me, to my mother, to my father and my brother and my two sisters, and that was all the stimulus I needed."

His youngest sister, Natasha, was reading very fluently well before she started school. She blossomed at school, was always 'razor-sharp' and confident and in the top groups. That is, until option time when she suddenly found herself in the CSE groups and not those for GCE, even though she had achieved a mark in the upper eighties in maths, for example. The effect on her was 'just incredible', to the point where she now badly lacks confidence as a 16 year-old. A pupil who could cope with the playground abuse to which she was submitted through being black, capitulated and turned in on herself. One of Kevin's most searching sculptures is called 'Why?' and is of a black questioning face sculpted when Natasha had been demoted into the lower examination groups. She has gone on to college at 16+ as Kevin did, and she looks set to obtain the examination results she should have achieved at school.

His elder sister, Denise, accepted white people "to the point where she didn't really accept us, her family, because we were black".

"It got to the point where she felt the need to be white, she felt so bad about being black. This really hit home one day. They used to play the game called 'Brown Girl in the Ring'. The kids used to do something really cruel. She'd be the brown girl in the ring and they'd taunt her and push her about and they'd actually use her in playing brown girl in the ring...later on she was in the same game again, but they did it in a more malicious way and it went home that she really was different."

The television drama 'Roots' led to her receiving taunts about slavery and there were anti-black slogans sprayed all over the school for "the National Front were riding high with all their propaganda" at the time. Denise found it all too much to contend with, and one day,

"Denise was upstairs and my mother went upstairs to see what she was doing. She heard Denise crying and went into the bathroom. Denise had Flash, bleach, Ajax and so on, and she was scraping her skin off. She'd scraped her skin off from her knuckles right up to her elbows on both arms, until they were just red raw, and she was crying like anything. It upsets me now, it upsets me every time I talk about it. My mother broke down and said to her, 'But why are you doing this?' And Denise said, 'Well, if I could get rid of this colour they wouldn't call me names anymore and they'll treat me just like the rest'."

Though Denise does modelling now, she cannot show her arms because of the disfiguring scars.

Kevin recalls in his own schooldays how he used to dread history lessons that were to do with black people.

"In school we have to put up with the degrading way that they deal with black history where the only things that you learn about your culture are that, 'They were in Africa and we made them civilised. We gave them this. We gave them religion. We taught them how to read and write. Before we came, they just swung through the trees. Before we came, they all had plates in their lips and they all had rings round their necks, you know! They were just so primitive. Now if you look at all that, you see, we've got them to where they are today!'"

However confident you are before you experience such attitudes and values, Kevin asks which black child is not going to come down or switch off in his or her studies. Like Natasha he also had the humiliating experience of being put in the CSE Art group, even though it was a subject in which he had always shown talent. He got the top grade in GCE, but had to enter by paying for himself.

These harsh experiences became the source of Kevin's work and a release, because when "I can't get hold of clay or a drawing board I start to revert to how I was before and I start to get bitter because I haven't got my work to release it, because my actual method of working is very expressive."

'On Being a Black Artist in Britain'

"Jim Robeson (my ceramics lecturer) wanted me to actually coil, because I was making heads about a metre or so high, and he said, 'Kevin, you are going through too much clay, coil it. You'll get just the same effect by coiling.' I tried it but when you are coiling you can't get a rolling pin and really be expressive and really show the anger that you feel, because if you bash it it's going to collapse and you're just going to have a heap of clay."

But "bash it" he continued to do, thinking about Natasha being put into the bottom group for maths,

"...or I think about when I was beaten up, or when I went for a job and they wouldn't let me have one because they saw the colour of my skin, or when I was put into a bottom group for subjects I knew I was capable of doing, or when I had to enter myself for Art...or even when we used to do sports, and I used to pick up the javelin and they'd say, 'Oh, you're natural at that, aren't you Kevin?' and things like that. I used to just think about those situations armed with the rolling pin. I felt I could get rid of all these feelings of anger and that was how I was able to start creating my sculptures."

In terms of what he was about, he feels that the actual working method had to convey the same kind of message as well; it would be "somewhat contradictory" to work in a "very light technical way on a piece that is supposed to be angry...It is like trying to paint a really angry expressive face on a piece of studio ceramics, or doing nice, tight fancy designs on a raku piece - it doesn't work".

"You have got to work with the medium and work with the expression you are trying to convey and the two have got to match...Once I've got that stimulus in mind, I have the block of clay, and the first thing I have to hack out is the neck. I beat it with the rolling pin and I get big chunks of clay and rip them off because obviously the neck is going to be somewhat thinner than the base of the head. Once that's been done, I start to whittle it down to the eyes, the nose...I never work against the medium by abusing it - I work with it...sometimes you can see a head in the block of clay before you've even touched it. It's like when you look at the clouds and you can see a face, well I get a similar thing when I look at clay."

Though he does not feel the need to make preparatory drawings, he will always work "with a mirror and make expressions into the mirror and copy them on

to the clay". He does not intend that his pieces are simply to be looked at.

"I like to make them very tactile. I think it's as important to get as much information from touching it as looking at it...I get so mad going into these galleries and they've got perspex boxes around the sculpture or they won't let you touch it, because I feel that it is very, very valuable to touch it, and that's why I like everyone to touch my pieces - not just look at them and just say, 'very nice'. I want them to get to grips with it and touch the whole thing."

Once the essential forms have been realised and Kevin is happy with the way it looks, he moves on to a stage where he textures the surfaces, acknowledging his debt to Jim Robeson in this respect - "Jim has got this off to a fine art."

"Now I work with textures in much the same way as a 2-D person works with pencils or pastel inasmuch that if you want to really heighten certain textures, if you want textures to really stand out, to really come forward, then you have to put a smooth area next to it. Likewise, when a person is doing a drawing and you really want a focal point to come out towards the viewer, then you darken the surrounding areas - then it really stands out and really hits home...That's how I work with clay and that's why I think that textures are so important."

When he is in full flow "people think I'm a bit demented", for he will grab lace, people's trainers, an item of clothing with good textures - anything that he thinks is relevant, he will push on to the clay.

"Then I'll roll out very fine bits to put against that, and the textures really come up. This is where oxides work really strongly because they really do pick out such textures...I use manganese dioxide to cover the whole thing, that's usually my base. Then I use wire wool or brillo pad, and take off the top surface...You actually highlight certain areas by taking the oxide (or the patina) off the surface. Then I put cobalt dioxide on to give like a blue, and then I'll use copper to give the green. I sometimes put veradium in - it doesn't always come out yellow but sometimes you get a yellowish tinge."

Though he has experimented quite successfully with dry glazes, he feels that glazes in general are quite inappropriate to his needs.

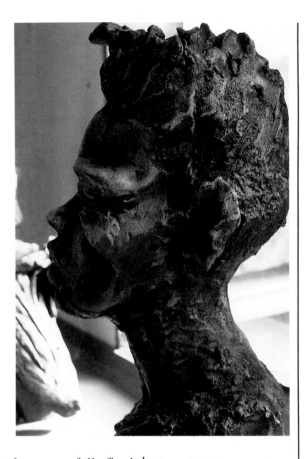

Kevin Johnson's presence in the Scheme contributed greatly to increasing pupil's understanding of the issues and concerns of life in a multicultural society.

'All around the studio are sculptured busts produced larger than life and in a strong, powerful style.'

A solid lump of clay cannot be successfully fired and at this stage, of course, Kevin's sculptures are still in the form of a block of clay so the next stage is crucial. He has to sense when the clay is at the right stage of hardness and then he slices the work into sections, hollows it out, re-assembles it and reworks the textures as necessary. He then forgets about it and gets on to the next piece. "That's why when you come to the school, you just see pieces that are, like, made and abandoned...By the time I've finished with that rolling pin and I've seen that expression I want, it's served its purposes, it's finished as far as I'm concerned." Eventually, of course, the piece is fired and the longer the delay, the more chance of any lingering air bubbles seeping out. He takes the kiln up to 500 degrees very slowly, and then goes rapidly up to 1200, normally without any problems because of the resilience of the heavily grogged craft crank clay he uses.

It is important to go through his working processes in some detail because these have evolved to be in keeping with the content and protest in his work, and it is the fusion of style and message which gives his sculptures their extraordinary power and impact. "I use my work to protect myself," he observes! He does not feel relaxed within the Wigan community. "Far from it."

"But there's a motto I go by. 'If I don't keep going and do what I do, I will always be going in

'I work with textures in much the same way as a 2-D person works with pencils or pastel': oxides are used to further highlight these textures.

through the back door.' Now, when I say the back door, I'm talking more about the Civil Rights movement that took place in America that was forwarded by Martin Luther King. Prior to the work he did, everything was segregated, as it still is in some parts of the world like South Africa. If they hadn't pulled together and said, 'I have as much right to this as you have. I have as much right to be here as you have. This is my country as much as it is yours.' If they hadn't done that, then things would be exactly as they were. We'd still be going through the back door."

Though he believes that things have changed for the better in the sense that "things have been a lot worse", he still finds himself subjected to considerable abuse. One man tried to run him down recently, people frequently wind down their car windows to hurl abuse at him and he knows to avoid certain pubs. "There's a part of me that wants to go to Manchester or another part of the country that's easier for black people, but there is also a part of me that wants to stay here because I have as much right to be here...I actually feel the need to go into white areas for that reason, rather than all black areas."

Kevin is a tall, striking looking young man with a personable manner, and he is a remarkable and articulate communicator. He has had a great impact on the school in which he is resident, and, as a result of his Grange-over-Sands presentation, has been

A dramatic arrangment of Kevin Johnson's ceramic sculptures in his studio during a primary residency.

Colin at work on a ceramic head against the imposing backdrop of one of Kevin Johnson's Amanda Faulkner-motivated pastel paintings.

A section of a display of ceramic heads by St John Fisher school pupils.

invited to speak in a number of schools. Having learned to control the anger he feels, he has made himself into an excellent ambassador for black people, as the responses of students from a sixth form college illustrate. (8)

"I thought he had a positive attitude towards racism, bringing out the racist remarks which were thrown upon him in his sculpture and painting work. I was surprised by how much he had to say (a lot!) on racism, and he went on and on with sculpture masterpieces which conveyed his torment. I was impressed by how he could stand in front of about 100 people and talk freely about his family, and the different episodes which occurred in his life. This would take a great deal of courage. He had come to a town known as 'the white ghetto' of Wigan. I had seen him afterwards at a bus station, and people not of his origin were

staring at him. He is so cool at how he handles his anger at people."

"After listening to his talk I felt guilty, not only for being part of a society which could be so cruel to racial minorities, but for such cruelty to anyone no matter what their background or beliefs. I had thought before that such inhumane behaviour was wrong but Kevin's talk really drilled home the message. It is really sad that minority groups can't feel proud to be who they are, that we should make them want to be white like us..."

"I was moved by the stories about his sister and her obsession with being accepted by whites that she went so far as to disfigure herself in an attempt to make herself white. The sculptures themselves were fantastic both in size and appearance. I loved the way he told us how he went about making them. Taking out his anger and emotion on them by beating, thumping and kicking them. The faces were amazing. You could see the different emotions in each of them - pain, suffering, proudness. They showed how although the blacks feel undermined by the whites, they know themselves they are equally important and proud of their race."

"I thought that in his sculpture of heads he captured very well the pain that blacks suffer. One particular sculpture of his mother seemed very insulting towards her but after his explanation I think it captured everything she must have endured in her life. Before his talk I would have never known black artists suffered any more prejudice than white artists."

"His work is relevant and extremely powerful in showing us for what we are and what we unknowingly do to others."

While in Wigan, a major new development has taken place in Kevin's work for, at Grange-over-Sands, he was deeply affected by Amanda Faulkner's presentation about her work and, indeed, by the works themselves when he was able to study them in her Drumcroon exhibition a few weeks later. Though he does not feel indebted to many artists, he admits to being 'greatly influenced' by Rodin - "I hold him up there!" - and a black artist, Bill Ming, has also been a profound influence. "His sculptures are amazing and he actually inspired me to take Art further." They still keep in touch. But at Grange-over-Sands in Amanda's talk,

"...the slides started to come up. I thought it was really, really good. I don't think I would have gleaned as much information if she hadn't given me such a very precise insight into her work. She

was so articulate...I got the impression she was holding nothing back - what you were getting was everything. I like that up-front kind of approach, she was able to talk about things that happened to her that seemed so private - and she was just able to blurt out the whole lot and she didn't care who was there. I had great respect and admiration for her, but most of all the way that it came out so strongly in her work. I had never seen pastels used in that way, so I was really taken."

However, he found himself also quite upset by her work, particularly her recurring use of red "reminded me of the menstrual cycle" and as he sat there his own half-buried memories of his childhood began to surface, "all these things rushed straight back", particularly memories of abuse he had suffered at the hands of a neighbour - a secret he had only recently confided to his mother.

"I straight away started to experiment with pastels but I made exactly the same mistakes, I now realise, that I made when I was at college. I latched onto her style, which is not me. That is Amanda Faulkner and that is special to her. That is why the first drawings were crap, basically, as good as I thought they were then."

They served an important purpose, though, that of enabling him to add a new medium in which to express himself. As this developed, his St John Fisher studio has taken on an increasingly dramatic appearance with the ceramic busts covering the whole workbench top along one length of the room and the pastels hanging like panels from the ceiling, the earliest smaller pieces on the walls above the workbench, two of which deal with the child abuse aspects. The visiting teacher's report says of them,

"His pastel drawings which were a recent diversion from his sculptures were rich in content and techniques, each contained a white caricature of himself and made a statement or disturbing personal recollections. The effect that this work had upon the pupils of the school was (that) clearly some had been prompted to work on a large scale in pastels with pleasing results." (9)

Kevin sees this development as a further illustration of just how valuable Art can be as a self-expressive medium and how important it is to the adolescent child.

"Now I'm 24, so if I can feel the need to express myself like that, then how much more should a

child who is going through so much emotional turmoil due to changing and so on, feel the need for expression through an artistic medium, which is why I cannot begin to understand why the government should choose to cut back on the Arts and Art time when in a child's education that time is invaluable."

In his own terms, he feels great respect and a great debt towards Amanda Faulkner because he does not believe that he would have started to draw again but for her, but in addition,

"It also helped me to get out of a rut with my ceramic pieces, because you fall into the danger of performing - producing a piece on demand. I can do it very easily. I can have a block of clay and have no feeling and - whumph - it's there, but they all look the same...I actually felt with the clay pieces, 'Oh, they're all looking the same'. But after Amanda, I had to take on something new and for the first time in a while it was a challenge."

Not only that, though, for in the process the pastel works also proved to be a regenerative spur to his claywork.

"I took on the pastels and then that character, the caricature of myself came out and, as you saw, that then fed back into the claywork and gave that new life. Now if I hit another rut, I will go to a new medium and then take it back into the clay again. So Amanda's helped me an awful lot, not just my drawing but also my ceramic pieces."

The 'caricature' was himself white amongst his black family and, though Kevin has reservations about living and working in 'white Wigan', his influence on many teachers and young people has already been considerable. The visiting teacher's report records that, "Kevin has extended his contact to the other staff of the school outside the Art department and the majority of the teachers in the school had attended in-service courses he had organised." Many young people have come to respect him as an intelligent, humorous and friendly artist and person in his own right. Colin, a fifth former with ideas about going into catering, illustrates the degree to which pupils have identified with him. Colin had no previous experience of using clay, but was soon building impressive, large scale pots, some with faces appearing out of the sides.

"It started six weeks ago when I first met Kevin and the exams were coming up, so I thought,

'pots, big pots'. The first one started going funny, but it straightened up after a bit. You have to keep standing back from the pot when you are coiling, and the coils were quite thick...Kevin's work is very good and I would like to be like Kevin in the way he can do Art, but I'll never be as good as that. I'm not really that good at Art - we'll have to see what happens!" (10)

Kevin definitely uses the 'front door' and effects change from the inside, just as his mother suggested he should. In the process, the impact which he has had in Wigan and the effects on numerous young people's thinking, indicates how important it is that the black artist works in all-white communities to modify attitudes, as well as in those with high Afro-Caribbean and Asian populations.

*Kevin Johnson designed
and made this skeletal
structure in sections to
help firing in the primary
school kiln, to aid
learning in the 'My Body'
project, and to make a
provocative statement
about being black in
Britain.*

7

The Enterprise Board Artists

Visiting teachers in Anne-Marie Cadman's Atherton Hindsford Primary School studio from which she conducted her business for two and a half years.

"I didn't have anywhere to work and I was worried that if I went for the Enterprise Board I'd lose too many months just looking for somewhere to work and I wouldn't benefit from the year's money. I'd gone to the Awareness Day quite in advance of applying for it - it was about three or four months before. But I kept thinking, 'Well, I can't apply for it yet because I've nowhere to work'. I couldn't see an end to it really!" (1)

After studying Textiles in higher education for four years, Anne-Marie Cadman found herself back home and on the dole. She wanted to work for herself and since about the Christmas of her final year at college had been carefully building up stock. She describes herself as being, at the time, rather timid with a tendency to put things off. Anne-Marie became Wigan's first Enterprise Board artist in February 1987, and pioneered such artists working within Wigan's schools: by Easter 1989 there were 12 artists funded through the Enterprise Scheme.

To qualify for this Scheme the artist has to have £1,000 in the bank. The artist then receives £40 a week for one year with a view to becoming estab-

▲ *An area of Anne-Marie Cadman's studio emphasises the bold and decorative use of colour and shapes which characterise her work.*

▼ *One of her distinctive lines are the felt hats, their shapes inspired by those worn by Thunderbirds puppets and Noddy.*

lished in business. In most cases the artists are financially worse off than on the dole, for the money they receive is more than gobbled up by the cost of their equipment and materials and other overheads, such as their travel costs between home and work or those incurred by getting their work into, for example, craft shops or fairs. Nevertheless, one or two of the artists who were able to work at home willingly came into Wigan schools because they found the loneliness and lack of contact with like-thinking people to be very real problems.

Anne-Marie Cadman is an important case study as the first Enterprise Board artist to work in a Wigan school and it is possible to follow her career in the year-plus since her Enterprise funding ceased.

"...I was worried about having nowhere to work. I knew I needed quite a bit of space and I had my eye on this little workshop which was an old stonemason's. I kept on walking there; it was empty, but I never plucked up the courage to knock on the door. I really wasted quite a lot of time worrying about what I was going to do. I'd tried a little bit of selling, I'd tried a few stalls to see what kind of reception I got and I'd also started doing little things at home, but I couldn't do anything big."

One Saturday in January 1987 she accompanied her mother to the library in Leigh. In the foyer she saw the poster advertising the Turnpike Gallery's exhibition of the Artists in Wigan Schools which had opened that morning.

"So I went up to see the exhibition and I was very impressed. I remember the big jacket that the student had made with Angela Cusani and the cows that some kids had done with Andy Shaw, and I thought that they were incredible. I remember some of Angela's own work too. I took a catalogue away and read it from cover to cover and I noticed this other place at the bottom - Drumcroon. So, very unusual for me, I got on the phone."

In response to her telephone call it was suggested that she brought along a portfolio, but to avoid building up false expectations it was clearly emphasised that, at least at present, no posts were available on the same basis as those artists who were represented in the Turnpike exhibition. However, Drumcroon staff were interested to know about any young artists who were living and working within the Wigan area.

"I was really nervous. I remember bringing my folder up here to the Drumcroon library and having all my work out on the floor and tables...and I just remember feeling very good and very positive. I'd had some very bad experiences and that was one of the first positive experiences I'd ever had of showing my work to people who were honest enough to tell me exactly what they thought."

Anne-Marie explained her dilemma about wanting to do the Enterprise year but fearing that if she applied she risked wasting precious months searching out somewhere to work and therefore losing the benefit of the year's money. Drumcroon offered her the opportunity of having a school-based studio, with the implication that she could apply to the Enterprise Board immediately.

"Well at first, I thought, 'Oh yes, that sounds really good'. But when asked what sort of school I would be most interested in, I thought, 'I don't really know,' because I hadn't had much contact with children and I always thought that I didn't get on very well with them. I could just think of little toddlers and not being able to communicate with them, but then I thought of secondary kids and, from my own experience, remember them tearing around everywhere. Then I really warmed to the idea and when we went down to the school in the afternoon it seemed right."

By the end of that afternoon all the details had been sorted out, it was agreed that Anne-Marie's studio would be an indoor playground area adjoining three teaching spaces in Atherton Hindsford Primary School, and she could immediately apply to the Enterprise Board. At first they were a bit sceptical about her using a school, but their attitudes changed once they realised she could be at the school as long as the caretaker was there and that he only had four weeks off in the year. It took quite a while for her to settle in and establish a satisfactory working routine, partly because she felt that she had to be careful to work "within the rules".

"With Enterprise there are all these little rules that you mustn't have been trading before and you mustn't be seen to be already in existence. So as soon as I am on day one I can start moving in. I didn't want anything to jeopardise it. I thought they might be thinking, 'Oh, watch this one and see what happens!' So as soon as I got the money, I started moving into the school."

The school was very helpful giving her tables, cupboards and the like. Then she started ordering equipment and grappling with decisions about whether she bought screens or made her own. It took her "a good six weeks to really get going" but then she remembers "it was just happening and I was working". At first it was rather lonely, though the head teacher used to come up quite frequently, then the children started to come in more and more as well as the other staff. The 50/50 principle, a fundamental feature of the Artists in Wigan Schools Scheme, was waived in Anne-Marie's case. In keeping with the spirit of the Enterprise venture, it was agreed that she spend all her available time on her own work in order to produce the necessary volume to establish herself in business. This meant that the staff kept a certain distance out of respect for what she was attempting to do. Once properly established, she ran two in-service courses, each of two hours a week for six weeks, for teachers and parents.

"I think it was doing those that made me closer to them because I think they realised that I was just like them and that I wasn't this trendy artist who had all these stupid ideas and thought she was better than everybody else. After I did the course...the staff really opened up. They started to come along and say, 'I've got this idea. Do you really think it will work? How can I make it a bit more interesting?'...I think they really wanted to ask me things all the time, but until they got to know me they felt they couldn't. After that it was great because I felt that I could just pop into a class and see what they were doing...and they were forever coming in and saying, 'I want to do this'. I liked that...one woman was really taken up with the way you can put more than one colour on and by using three colours with the squeegee straight onto the material you get these really

beautiful marble-type effects. It was bonfire night so she had this idea of doing the fire. All the children worked on the material with the inks to try and get these fiery effects, and that was with reception children."

They began to pick up on the things Anne-Marie was doing. In one class children painted and printed inks onto fabric to create a dragon's body. As part of another project about a house which the children had wired up so that it could be lit up, it was decided that curtains were needed for the windows, "so every child in that class came and printed a little pair of curtains to put up".

To overcome that initial settling in period, would it have been better to start off with, say, a morning or afternoon a week with the children? Anne-Marie found that there were times when she was under such pressure to get orders out that this would have proved difficult, but on the other hand when she was well on top of the commercial side she would willingly have worked with teachers who were deliberately leaving her alone.

"It's no great impingement really, but I always felt and still do feel that, apart from being very grateful, that you must give something back and I work with them whenever I can. I'd like to work with them more, but there are times when I just can't because I have deadlines to meet."

However, a nominal contact time negotiable between herself and the head teacher would certainly have been beneficial and helped overcome her initial feelings of isolation, she believes. Her 12 months were completed at the end of February 1988. In the month between then and Easter in-service funding enabled her to work officially throughout the school on the same basis as the other members of the Artists in Wigan Schools Scheme.

"It was hard because it was only three days a week for four weeks and I really wanted to get a lot done. I really worked the children hard. I had to work within a school topic which I didn't want to do at first because I had this idea of what I wanted to do. The head teacher said that they were doing 'under the ground'. One class was doing under the ground about jewels, others were doing burrowing animals and some were doing fossils. But it was having this put upon me, because I could only do so much with the topic. Having said that, though, they did produce some brilliant work - I was really pleased."

Hindsford primary pupils working in Anne-Marie Cadman's studio.

To round off the term the school organised an exhibition of the work which had been produced and invited parents and other guests. The whole school was alive with the children's work: handmade paper pieces, made by individuals and groups, large and small; large textile panels with boldly painted and printed designs, others of a more constructional nature hanging from the ceiling; every area of the school reflected the intensity of that month's activity. At the centre of it was Anne-Marie's studio in which all her wares were superbly displayed resulting in her making many sales.

Having completed her Enterprise year she continued to use her studio in the school spending, in all, two years and five months there, at which point circumstances caused her to move out of the area.

"Because I'd had a week with each class, I got to know all the kids really well. Some of them, especially the top juniors, I hadn't had much contact with because they were quite a way from my work area, but after that they'd knock on the window when they were in the playground because they could see me, and then they'd come in."

She feels that she is doing quite well in business terms, but is fully aware that three to five years are required to become fully established. On the day she brought her portfolio to Drumcroon she was promised first option on a place within the Artists in Wigan Schools Scheme, but twice turned down such offers.

"If I'd never started off in business, yes, I would have preferred to become one of the mainstream artists. When you first offered me a place I felt very guilty because part of me really wanted to say yes, but I wanted to give the business my best shot, and it would have been awful to give it up and never know what I could have achieved. When you made me a later offer, again it was the same decision because by then things had taken off quite well. Each month I have increased sales and I seem to have more opportunities, I seem to be doing more."

However, one of the artists who worked at Drumcroon on Saturday mornings left, and Anne-Marie readily took her place and proved an ideal person to work with school groups when it became necessary to appoint somebody for one day a week. An unhappy experience, though, was that of working for one day a week in a technical college in a neighbouring authority. Though she made a number of friends amongst the staff, she didn't like the atmosphere there because some appeared to dislike the students and were very unkind to them. In addition,

The school foyer area decorated with the pupils' handmade paper pieces.

Anne-Marie Cadman discussing her work with a visiting group of pupils during the 'Connections' exhibition at Drumcroon.

A member of the Drumcroon staff making use of Anne-Marie Cadman's ideas books in her 'Connections' exhibiton area.

▲ Art college students studying Anne-Marie Cadman's ideas books during 'Connections'.

"...nobody spoke to me and I didn't know what I was supposed to be doing...but I got on great with the students because I just treated them like I'd treat anybody else. I actually saw situations where, because they didn't like a student, they slagged her work off, but I thought the work was certainly not as bad as that of somebody else who was being praised...I saw one girl reduced to tears just because of a personality clash."

Anne-Marie began to "dread going in", feeling that she could not handle this unfortunately all too common scenario at this stage of education.

She needed some extra work once the Enterprise year was over, but she found two days a week too much of an interruption to her business, so was relieved to give up the technical college day anyway. She feels that she is going to have to kick into touch some of her 'lines' because they are becoming too many and varied. As a continuation from college she started off with headscarves and hats.

"Then I thought, 'Well, these are a bit dear. I'll have to bring some small items in, some cheaper items,' and then I started with cards, a little bit of jewellery, and it started developing after that. Some men had been coming up to me and saying, 'Oh, you don't do anything for men. You go on about men being sexist!' So I started doing ties and bow ties."

Using her computer prints left over from college she started making pictures by reprinting them and framing them up and then, to make them more interesting, she began ripping them up and collaging them. On one of the monthly in-service days for the artists she experimented with the machine embroidery techniques used by Isobel Smith.

"I feel that's a real progression in my work, because although it's very textured and reasonably rich, it's got a certain flatness about it which, by taking it into embroidery makes it much more three-dimensional and gives it more depth."

She enjoys making small things and doesn't repeat herself much, but unfortunately, because of their price she does not sell many large works.

"I absolutely love doing those big felt wall hangings and painted hangings...I like nothing better than having a huge piece of material laid out on the table. I think secretly there's always been a painter trying to get out of me, because I've always liked paintings and I've always liked huge pieces of paper and I've wanted to spend more time painting. That's been released now through my textiles."

A high-point of her time spent in Wigan was the invitation to be one of four artists who would form the Drumcroon 'Connections' exhibition, her Conference Room space in the building being ideal for the presentation of her larger works.

"I remember when I was first asked to do that I was really flattered, I suppose, because I wasn't a 'proper' mainstream artist, I was an Enterprise artist. I felt a bit guilty because I didn't have a lot of children's work. So I had mixed feelings. I felt a bit of a fraud because I didn't have the same elements as the others had."

In the event, the children's works looked superb in the company of Anne-Marie's felted, printed and painted textile pieces. Though she is rather retiring by nature, the 'Connections' catalogue captures something of the bold nature of her work. (2)

"Strong decorative features figure prominently in her work but she often contrasts busy, intermingled and colourful backgrounds with superimposed shapes, like spirals, zig-zags and triangles which are dark and flat...The colours are invariably strong, vibrant and evocative of her formative years, as can be seen in many of the accessories that she makes which are designed to be bold, distinctive and fun to wear. As she says, 'I used to love pink fluorescent tee-shirts and I had all the (punk) stuff. I'd just go around the shops and buy anything bright that I could alter. I love brash things and I love kitsch things'."

In contrast to her initial apprehensions about young children,

"...I've really enjoyed working with children. I've found that they are capable of a lot more than I'd given them credit for...and they have some really good ideas as well."

Casting her mind back to that day when she plucked up the courage to phone Drumcroon,

"...I think I've got much more faith in myself than I had at the time. I've had a lot of different experience, like working with teachers and working with children, and then working here at Drumcroon where you are talking to people, which is a very good confidence-boosting exercise

for me...I feel very fortunate and I also feel very grateful for all the support and encouragement that I've had. I feel part of the Artists in Wigan School Scheme even though I'm not properly part of it. If I hadn't stumbled across here, then I would just have got a room somewhere...I wouldn't be in the position that I am in today and at the moment I feel very confident!"

In return, Anne-Marie Cadman has contributed far more to the Wigan Service than just being a school-based artist attempting to establish herself in business. Though quiet and unassuming, her presence has been felt in many aspects of the Service and her influence on teachers has been such that large num-bers of pupils have been affected, directly and indi-rectly, through the processes, values and qualities embodied in her work and through her personal qualities.

Eight months into Enterprise she was joined by the ceramicist, Kim Davies, who had been a techni-cian at Hawkley Hall High School. The then head of Art and Design felt very strongly that Kim's talents were being under-used and it was with her support and not a little persuasion that Kim came back to the school as an Enterprise artist. She worked there for two years, after which she obtained a place on a PGCE course. Anne-Marie and Kim became friends and have teamed up to show their work at trade fairs.

Since 1987 Drumcroon has received a steady

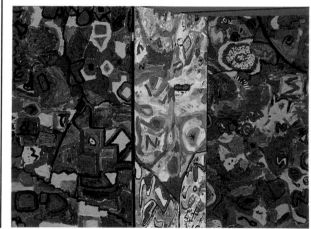

This boldly coloured and patterned screen was displayed in 'Connections'.

A rich cross-section detail of the screen made by the junior pupils.

A screen made by Hindsford junior pupils and one made by infants in the background.

stream of enquiries, letters, slides and curriculum vitae from artists learning about the Scheme by word of mouth and anxious to find employment. Though these were obviously well in excess of the posts available, some took up the offer of having studios in schools on an unpaid basis along with advice on how they might approach the Enterprise Board.

In consequence, the number of artists working in Wigan increased to about 30 on occasions, with this complementary aspect to the Scheme adding a new and enriching dimension. The Prince's Trust Award provided one artist with the necessary £1,000 to qualify for an Enterprise placement, while a painter already working at home on the Enterprise Allowance came into a school to work. One artist had to travel from Manchester each day, and found the discipline of having to arrive at the start of the school day beneficial. Inevitably, though, some Enterprise residencies foundered for financial reasons, travelling expenses were too high for the paltry £40 a week. One artist never started, even though her school had been carefully identified, she had visited it, and come to thank us as the Enterprise representatives had congratulated her on the clarity of her intent. Yet another withdrew after one term saying that she begrudged the time spent with pupils - minimal though this was in her case; a rare illustration, in our experience, of an artist who needed to work in private.

The Enterprise aspect of the Wigan Scheme is one which can be replicated by any local authority or group of schools with the necessary will, as the main ingredient is not finance but support. Indeed the Hindsford head teacher maintains that, in the light of Anne-Marie Cadman's residency, her preference would be for another Enterprise artist in the future.

"...if you have an artist-in-residence you always feel you have to use them all the time and I feel we've used Anne-Marie when we've needed her, we haven't felt compelled. Because she's joined in as part of the school, it hasn't put people on the defensive...the children see her as part of the school and use her work as part of their everyday work. Now I feel that if we'd had an artist-in-residence there'd have been more of a push to use that artist. This way she's been used more freely...but with Anne-Marie she's been so busy anyway doing her own things that she's been a bonus." (3)

During the course of the residency a new deputy head teacher has been appointed to the staff who believes that "Art comes into everything. It's a large chunk of my philosophy...Children learn through it,

they really do, because they're actually involved, it's a physical thing...It's cross-curricular but it stands in its own right as well". She rapidly developed a close working relationship with Anne-Marie, in addition she likes

"...the open door idea. Anne-Marie is working in there all the time, but the door is always open and the children are aware of what she is doing all the time...there's quite a large number who are interested in what she is doing and are always popping in to see. And they are very aware of the way she works, and the influence does come out in their work with no discussion about what she's doing - we're not trying to link it with Anne-Marie, but the influence is there, it cannot help but be there. You can't get away from pattern, colour and texture.

I get on very well with Anne-Marie. We talk about lots of different things and she now comes to me and says, 'Will you just come over here? What do you think I should do to that?' So we've got a two-way thing. It's a partnership. I've been discussing what we are doing at the moment and she's been coming up with suggestions." (4)

Anne-Marie clearly demonstrates the impact that the Enterprise artist can have on a school. How many artists of similar abilities are there around the country who could benefit from such support while giving to others?

8

Sixth Form College Pioneering Initiatives

"The Art department has come through a complete metamorphosis from an ugly, almost motionless growth to a delicately designed butterfly...Since Christmas '85 Art has become more exciting and enjoyable. The atmosphere is comfortable, very unlike a 'lesson'...The students are more relaxed and air their views, discussing with their teachers rather than being told what to do and left to do it, whether they like it or not."
(1)

Angela Cusani in residence at Winstanley College: the embroidery behind her is now owned by the College and is one of a number of original purchases.

Jen conjures up a picture of the dramatic changes which have taken place during her time as a student at Winstanley Sixth Form College. In a short period the new head of Art and Design wrought changes which emphasised to Jen what she had previously been denied; she is now determined to undertake a compensatory third year at the College. During that year the residency of Angela Cusani ensured further development of the department; students today are still benefiting without having even met Angela. By the end of her year in residence the new ethos was so firmly in place that regression was inconceivable. Another student, Kathleen, desribes the importance of the changes which were

"...for the better, because there just seemed to be one thing going on two years ago - traditional drawing. Everybody did the same project, and now its three-dimensional - there are so many! Angela has added another dimension to the department, so there are plenty of things going and we can all relate to each other and we are all inspired by each other." (2)

The residency became a perfect example of the partnership principles, arising partly out of the mutual understanding which already existed between head of department and artist, for one had taught the other at the A-level stage some years earlier at the neighbouring sixth form college, St John Rigby. The Winstanley College principal had also once taught there and was fully conscious of its Art and Design activities.

"...a vibrant department in which the kids had the light of battle in their eyes. Art mattered to them! They would describe themselves as artists while they were still at school. It was a wholly consuming occupation...there were a lot of kids who you might call 'artistic', they had been touched by an artistic experience." (3)

He wanted the same kind of "transfer of enthusiasm" from adult to student and a similar "injection of energy" at Winstanley College. Both were to become everyday features in Art and Design during that crucial year.

In the week before the new term, the head of

department and Angela began to discuss the setting up and workings of the residency. Angela's preparations were of a practical nature,

"...for the different things like weaving, machine embroidery and papermaking, I knew I would go into some depth. I also set up an environment for the students. We set up a little exhibition in the entrance hall and also set up the studio space (in the department) so that when the students came into college, whether they were Art students or not, they would know the type of work that I was involved in and what they would be involved with later in the term." (4)

The environments had the desired impact, a characteristic of all Angela's previous residencies. As at Golborne, she made use of the Tadek Beutlich weavings from the Schools Loan Collection. The colours and textures of her own work set off against the materials in her studio space foreshadowed future works. On returning for the third year, Jen recalls that,

"...the first impact was of colour, and that introduced me more to colour and texture with the weavings and the paperworks with their coloured bits of material and built-up textures in embroidery."

Stimulated to work in a similar way herself, Jen's work was to develop significantly during the year,

"...because I've always liked colour and texture and I think I draw in a textural way. What I wanted to do was to combine Textiles and Fine Art without losing any of the drawing or letting textiles take over. I think I achieved that!"

Feelings of kinship soon developed between Angela and the students for, being so young, they felt she was almost one of them. Partly because they naturally called her by her first name, but also because, "she's not a teacher, she's not a student - she's someone else, she's an artist-in-residence" who didn't have to take registers or do the other chores of teaching; "Why weren't you in? What were you doing? Will you please let me know? And why are you late?

Things like that...it's a middle line, in between." She was also privileged in the sense that she worked with smaller groups than the teachers and, very rapidly, she became the centre of a group of practitioners who worked together at lunch times and other spare moments. During the previous year it had become natural to work at lunch times, whereas in the past the department had operated strictly within working hours, and Angela helped to 'firm up' this process.

"We feel as though we want to come back now, not just pack our bags and walk out at the end of the lesson at dinner time, or something like that, which we always used to do before. It was just another lesson: you came in and sat down and doodled around on a piece of paper for a while, went out and that was it." (5)

By comparison, Angela's area helped to bond significant friendships as well as being a creative focal point, as Kathleen said,

"We would never have got together if it had not been for Angela - I met Debbie through doing the weaving with Angela, and Robert was there at the time doing the print and Jen the batik. We all began together and we've all stuck together, and that's because of Angela."

However, Robert emphasises that there "has to be a boss", and the head of department fulfilled that function, "you have got to provide a structure for it to work". A new teacher had commenced her teaching career on the same day that Angela started, and,

"It was quite an eye-opener for me. Nothing on teaching practice had introduced me to the idea of a working artist in the Art department. I didn't expect the department to look like it did: Angela's work area added something new.

I use Angela all the time, rather than just describing a technique I can show the students. They can see that you have to work hard to produce art and I don't just have to tell them it's hard work and they must keep going - they can see!" (6)

The artist's presence in the College was advertised in

Debbie wearing a 'mother earth' dress made for her to wear in a college drama production.

Robert working on a large handmade paper construction using processes introduced into the College by Angela Cusani.

Debbie using mixed-media processes while Angela Cusani works in the background.

Renu wearing her salvaar kameez made during her third year sixth studying art. As a non-art student she had begun to work with Angela Cusani at lunch-times.

the College Bulletin along with an invitation to non-Art students to come and work with Angela at lunch-times. This idea was to have a dramatic effect on the life of Renu, who, having made a blouse as a consequence of responding to that invitation, eventually stayed on for a third year sixth just to study Art and Design, in marked contrast to her previous maths and two science courses. It is her intention to go on to Art College to study Fashion and Textiles, a field in which she now demonstrates exceptional talents. She has become a much more relaxed and happy person as a consequence of this subject change.

In keeping with the Artists in Wigan Schools guidelines, Angela had a timetable devised on the 50/50 principle, but her popularity and concern for what the students were doing guaranteed that her own working time was under constant threat. By a certain stage in the residency, this problem began to resolve itself. She learned to make constructive use of rare slack periods and proved herself to be well-organised in preparing for the next day, and, because she was willing to support them, the students became increasingly sensitive to her needs,

"...she shows us she's not just here for us...all her time is not our time. We want to have some time to ourselves and when we see Angela doing that, it makes you realise that everybody needs time for themselves...but Angela's terribly patient with us. She's always there, really, even when it's her own time." (7)

Another student was conscious of a reciprocal process,

"It helps with Angela doing her own work because she can mix with the students and she can pick up ideas from them...she can tell you more information than a teacher could. A teacher has to look after the students, and they're not doing their own work so they're not finding ideas as much as Angela. It's really refreshing, so I think it's a good idea having these artists-in-residence."

A very important role which artists-in-residence fulfil is that of revealing to others the actual processes involved in the making of art,

"...they are seeing me as a communicator and seeing me as an artist who has got problems like they have with their work, then it brings them down to the level that they're just like an artist themselves. I think that's good to see because a lot of people think an artist cannot do anything wrong, that the results are always brilliant. I like

to think it's important that I admit in some areas that I don't know what's going on and it does make me think more...I like it best when the actual students come up and see my work and make a comment on my ideas."

To help these kinds of interactions and future developments, the head of department

"...ensured that enough students in the present Lower Sixth spent enough time with Angela for them to learn her skills but also to 'feel' the industry and her enthusiasm for the work. At this age students learn so much from one another." (8)

The residency became a good example of give-and-take, with Angela's contribution and impact unmistakeable, but with her in a learning situation also as she sought to relate what she had on offer to the College's Art and Design approaches. The head of department observes,

"We work well together; I hope we dovetail. She provided something exciting and a new approach to colour but she also had to fit in with the values of the course, already established. I like the students to spend time investigating and going into depth and she took some time seeing the relevance of this to a Textiles experience. Eventually she did - for we discussed the matter, and now she admits that she can see the benefits of this approach. She even says that it has opened her eyes and she now researches deeper herself..."

This combination of sketchbook investigation and the multi-discipline offered by Textiles began to give the work special characteristics.

Like the students, the head of department was sensitive to the distinct role of Angela,

"I feel sometimes that what I do is spread thin and that she is able to go into depth, and I know the importance of experiences in depth, not only on the technical side, but by allowing students time for investigation and experimentation and providing the continued support. I like to do this but sometimes I get distracted by other matters and feel torn and harassed."

Such is the lot of many teachers today with the pressures imposed on them by external duties increasing at such a rate that it is becoming an all too rare luxury to be able to teach with a sharp focus, unfettered by other distractions. Angela had been considering teaching as a career, but this residency gave her a clear picture of the problems. Instead she undertook an MA in Textiles to better equip herself to set up in business operating from home. As an artist-in-residence she was conscious and grateful that she was freed from all the constraints and pressures the staff had to cope with.

"...and the administration, I mean I don't have that at all...I've got the time to spend with one student if they come in their free time or lunch-times. If they want to do, say, a batik I can just go right the way through with them without any intrusion...As artists we can do our own work and I don't think we've got, maybe, the same discipline problems that teachers have, being involved with a fewer number of pupils."

In the previous two years in the Scheme, Angela's work had developed significantly from college days, and a commission for her to make a set of pieces for the Turnpike Gallery's Textiles and Ceramics 'Surface to Surface' exhibition had added a richly textured set of her works to the Wigan Schools Loan Collection, one of which was 'Turkish Delight'. At Winstanley, she was conscious of further important developments taking place.

"When I look back at 'Turkish Delight', the work that I'm doing now is like an extension of that but there are painterly elements. I'm using the dyes like inks, I'm using inks like paint, I'm painting with the print. I'm not only just using embroidery which I put with paper. Now there's more...It's become very much more intricate, and there's more depth and investigative work."

She also feels that she has picked up on Art History aspects of critical studies, extending her own knowledge in the process.

"The history thing, as well, while I've been here has been great for my own work. It's made me look more..."

She feels that she has a good knowledge of Impressionism, Fauvism and of contemporary artists who have influenced her own work, but feels she lacks education in this respect, particularly with regard to earlier Art,

"...that's an area that I know that I could just pick up on but not in a lot of depth, and I know for a fact that the other artists, like Philip Smith - he's the same. We know certain areas and a bit about others, but we don't know the whole lot in depth."

She feels that it has helped working alongside students who "have to put a lot of investigating and study into a subject". The students are encouraged to keep sketchbooks which they use regularly and rigorously as part of their studies, underpinned by a strong drawing course. Many of the most exciting developments during Angela's residency came about as students brought together her processes and ideas with their drawing and sketchbook approaches. Jen, for example, developed a regard for the Pre-Raphaelite painters "mainly because of their jewel-like colours and their immaculate detail" following a London visit, but also,

"Working closely with Angela, my interest for a Textiles approach grew. I wanted to combine Textiles approaches along with decorative detailed drawings, without one or the other taking over. I have tried to put this across in my recent work." (9)

A major outcome of this approach was a triple portrait, featuring a husband, wife and mistress caught up in the eternal triangle, giving her work a "moralistic view...in keeping with the Pre-Raphaelite approach". She found this work both enjoyable and a challenge and it

"...allowed me to express myself in two areas which I enjoy - Textiles and detailed observational drawing. These two aspects are very often separated. Also a piece of work on this scale allowed me to incorporate different techniques, such as printing, batik, knitting and emboss."

Prior to Angela's residency there had been no history of textiles in the College's Art and Design courses, but this use of drawing values combined with her techniques and approaches brought about an explosive, creative fervour in a wide variety of media. Kathleen writes,

"In my previous work I've liked to involve texture with paint and doing a weaving makes it possible to get in touch with surfaces, rough, smooth, holey, soft, spikey and to organise them into a composition that suggests a particular theme...At the moment the appearance of the work is fairly busy but big and thick - in other words, I want to sew on, tie on all the little details, little intricacies such as filaments and stamens, antennae and wings, tiny bobbles and buds inside, and on the larger flower forms I want to make the effect finer and more delicate...I am trying to keep to my ideas. I have my sketchbook studies out when I

work and refer to them regularly. The garden theme to me is working...I'm very glad of my little sketchbook now...I wanted to use, as near as possible, all natural materials - sisal, wool, fleece, string, cotton and raffia, etc. Now and then I dye the wool and raffia and the material strips." (10)

In a similar vein, Debbie describes her use of fabrics processes enlivened by the use of the sketchbook.

"My own sketchbook began with a drawing of my goldfish, 'Chester', done with wax crayons, blusher brushes and highlighters. I was fascinated by the reds, oranges, yellows and pinks which

sheets of his own handmade paper, overcoming considerable technical problems in the process, and allowing the paper's colouring to influence his choice of ink colours. He acknowledges Angela's contribution,

"She's helped a lot on the technical side of colouring, the matching up of colours and adapting these to different materials." (12)

One large print of the landscape from the Art room window led to further innovations as Robert incorporated actual grasses into his paper to combine with those which were cut into the block, and he went on

Jen discussing with high school visitors her attempts to reconcile Pre-Raphaelite qualities with Angela Cusani's broader use of media and processes.

The rich studio environments of Robert and Jen during the post A-level student residencies.

Michael's area was cool and understated, but visitors were drawn in because of the intensity of his drawings. Two fourth year high school pupils worked in his studio for a full week.

seemed to mingle as the fish moved. From this one study the ideas flowed and I found myself using all kinds of media: netting, onion bags, gold/yellow and white packing from melons (which I got from work) incorporated with silver buttons, wool and material, all the time stretching the idea and working the colours in." (11)

Amongst numerous studies, these, too, eventually led to a colourful and richly textured weaving.
    Relief printing had been introduced into the College by the head of department, but even the woodblock printing took on new dimensions during Angela's residency. Robert began printing onto large

to make paperworks with added materials as works in their own right.

Alan used batik as the basis for a large, irregularly shaped soft sculpture and Vicki, as a holiday project made a beautiful art history book out of handmade paper, the individual pages of which were embellished with rose petals, and the like. Sam made a coat with machine embroidery on the lining and sketches of a box of cress provided the basis for the boldly embroidered pockets and collar. At A-level time the students' Art and Craft studies fully reflected the vitality which had entered into the course during the year.

The head of department says of the residency,

"Overall the effect both on students and staff was amazing. We all became much more open and receptive. I know I learnt a lot; especially the new techniques which Angela brought into the department. It is easy to pick up on techniques and you are stupid if you don't pick the brains of the artist."

She was keen to ensure that the benefits of the residency continued after Angela had left, and picking up on the processes and techniques was the easiest and most obvious thing to do. Another important way was through the students, and that is why she ensured that sufficient numbers of the Lower Sixth came into contact with Angela, in the hope of a carry-over into the next year. For example, Caroline was using and developing the papermaking and embroidery processes 12 months later, taking them in unexpectedly new directions, as her description of some of the techniques used in her 'Shell Bay' panel indicates,

"The shell moulds were made by painting latex onto the shell and letting it set. Then I peeled off the mould. Into the mould I placed paper pulp of different colours or I dyed the pulp once it was in the mould. Then I squeezed the pulp into the mould to get the surface impressions of the shell. This was then left to dry. Once it was dry I coloured the paper shell with Caran D'Ache pencils and sewed it with threads and beads." (13)

Like Renu, Caroline stayed on for a third year sixth and both ensured that qualities from Angela's residency continued to be used and developed well beyond the residency: they can now be seen as a natural part of the department's repertoire two years after.

One major innovation, with far reaching implications, was the College implementing its own residency schemes, with the College's own students as the artists. The head of department explains,

"...the idea of residencies in our own department, basing them on the principles of the Wigan Scheme. Six of our Upper Sixth students who had left returned after their exams in June to work at their chosen craft within the department for two weeks. As well as the learning situation for them, acting as artists, they taught or 'communicated' with the Lower Sixth students. It also worked as a liaison exercise with pupils from our feeder schools, who came to view or work. We tried to demonstrate as many disciplines of Art and Design as we could."

The first year Angela was still there in her studio space, and the students created studio areas of similar size. One 11-16 high school sent three pupils to work alongside them throughout one full week, while other schools brought groups for half or whole days, each student describing and demonstrating what he or she did with practical activities on offer for the visiting pupils. The head of department saw the residencies as significant learning experiences for the students,

"The students who worked as artists enjoyed their new role and it was a good way of them carrying on with their work as a preliminary to going on to do Art and Design in higher education. They each set up an environment in the manner of Angela and brought in stimulus material as she did. All I did was co-ordinate the event; the students ran it after that."

As well as pupils from other schools, the entire London University Institute of Education PGCE Art and Design Course, lecturers and students, also visited. Jen talked to them with extraordinary aplomb, showing them reproductions such as the 'Ophelia' painting by Millais to illustrate the Pre-Raphaelite qualities which she had attempted to incorporate into her own work. They were so affected by the experience that the lecturers arranged a repeat visit for their PGCE students of the following year; it is to continue on an annual basis.

As well as high school groups, a number of primary schools came to see the residencies in operation the second year. In one hectic workshop session Alan, one of that year's student-artists, saw all the found objects he had laboriously collected for use in his assemblage sculptures completely absorbed into the young children's constructions, all of which were proudly carried away to be displayed in

*Julie's former high
school teacher working
alongside her in her
studio three years after
having taught her.*

*A fourth year high school
pupil working from a
posed model in Julie's
area.*

One young pupil capturing a complex pose.

their school. The head teacher of Nicol Mere Primary School visited with his children, second year juniors, and recalls,

"There was a wide variation of work and media. We stayed probably a couple of hours and looked at everything and talked about everything - and the communication! The eighteen year-olds explaining to the children what they were doing, and how they were doing it, was good, I thought, because it gave them a chance to decide what they were doing in their own minds." (14)

His own children took everything in, but without initially being 'noisy or enthusiastic' in any obvious outward way.

Third year junior pupil residencies provided some children with their first opportunities to draw from the posed figure.

Julie believed that Anne-Marie Quinn's controversial pastels helped some students come to terms with their own sexuality. The pencil drawing (right) is an A-level work of Anne-Marie's, now in the Schools Loan Collection.

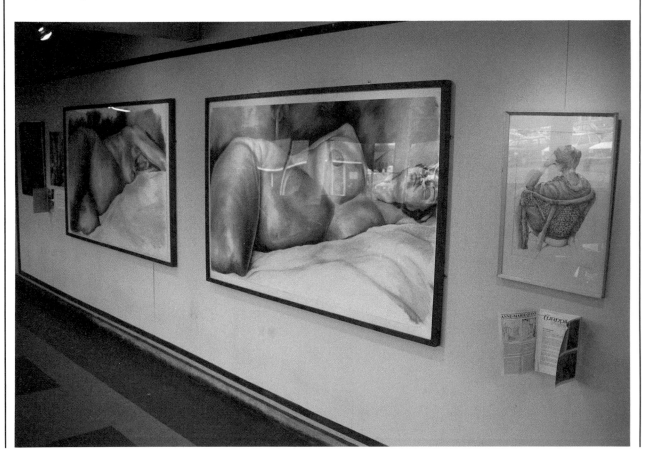

"They were a bit overawed for a time and then they relaxed and started to chat to the students, and there was a rapport between the two - I mean, you are talking about eight year-olds and eighteen year-olds. Now that is quite a big age gap. When you take them to a museum you are always a bit worried about how to get them to take it on board and participate. Now, with this I didn't have to do anything. It gelled and took over. It generated its own enthusiasm. I've never seen the like before."

The accompanying class teacher followed up the visit on the return to school, and,

"...they did some drawings and talked about it and wrote about it, and it was obvious they'd taken an awful lot in...I think there should be more of that kind of thing, not only in Art but in other subjects, because I think that if you got that going you would then get a spin-off and things would grow."

During the third year of the residencies the numbers of primary groups increased considerably, with the head teacher from the above school making an additional visit with a group of his staff and the technician, using the wide variety of stimulus on offer as a basis for a special and invaluable form of INSET. One primary class divided into three groups for practical work, having first talked with the artists about their displays. Some drew the figure, a sixth former posing for them. Others printed while the remainder built assemblage sculptures with Alan, who was one of two students who chose to participate. They had returned to the College having done their General Art and Design (GAD) year at the local technical college, prior to going on to BA Honours courses.

Even before the second year of the student residencies, the head of department was considering how the kind of stimulus which Angela had brought could be introduced by other means, with a little initiative and imagination.

"I will always encourage past students to return to College and display their work here and speak about their work to the students. If I can, I will try to give past students some space to set up their environments, though that will be difficult given the limited space I have in the department."

The necessary space was nevertheless found for Julie, who, having gone on to study a Multi-Arts course in higher education, had returned to the College to get together a portfolio having realised that she really wanted to study Art and Design at BA Honours level.

"Presently I have one student who did A-level here last year and wasn't enjoying her higher education course. She asked me if she could return and just work in the studio. So now she's set up - like a mini-residency. So you see, there are one or two ways of developing the idea."

In the event, two former students of the head of department also worked during the second year's residencies and, of course, a key environment and studio space was that of Julie who, during the year, had produced a series of larger-than-life size figures, some in pencil and others broadly painted. These built on her A-level course, during which she wrote, "like working big now...am doing a watercolour and pastel picture A1 size and a charcoal development of it in twice A1 size". All her work was of the figure, and her favourite artists were Degas and Mary Cassatt. These loves had initially been formed at her 11-16 high school when Anne-Marie Quinn was artist-in-residence there. The school's head of department brought a group of fourth form pupils to the residencies and he drew alongside Julie in her studio space while the pupils also worked from the same model in pastel; there was the intriguing situation of her former teacher working in her studio on her terms from subject matter developed from the stimulus of an artist who had been resident in his department.

Not only that, but while Julie was an A-level student two large pastels of a pregnant nude by Anne-Marie belonging to the Wigan Schools Loan Collection were displayed in the Winstanley College foyer area, generating a great deal of heated debate, argument, embarrassment and hostility. Already a great admirer of Anne-Marie's work, Julie got a tremendous amount from them, as did numerous other students. In an extended piece of writing Julie makes the observation that in the whole series (there are about eight pastels in all) Anne-Marie uses the same model "enabling one to find an intimacy with the model", just as Mary Cassatt had done after 1900 through repeated use of the same models. Fully conversant with the content, form, process, mood model, Julie goes on to capture the mood of these large pastels,

"On looking at the paintings I get a warm feeling which is quite hard to describe - it is as though I am happy for the model and can feel the empathy that Anne-Marie had with her. The works directly affected me, mainly because of the subject matter, but also because they are such bold statements.

*The paintings are quiet, soothing and relaxed. The
mood is very peaceful and tranquil and the subtle
colour scheme and soft pastels contribute to this
effect. This mood is also conveyed because the
model is asleep and lying horizontally
(symbolising calm)...One almost feels the relief of
her lying with the lump on her side and because
the paintings are so arresting and powerful all
distractions and sounds around me seemed to
disappear." (15)*

She comments on the taboo nature of the subject and
that the few pregnant nudes in art are normally
standing upright because "people think they suggest
eroticism if they are horizontal".

*"...which is exactly what happened when Anne-
Marie's paintings were displayed in the foyer at
College last year. There were comments flying
about like 'I can't eat my dinner anymore in front
of these disgusting pictures'. However, when
people began to discuss the paintings with each
other, the crisis began to die down. Most people
realised that it wasn't the paintings but it was
themselves having to come to terms with their own
sexuality."*

One thing to do with these paintings which Julie
thinks is wonderful is that "since being completed,
Anne-Marie herself has experienced the feelings
that her model, Tessa, felt as she has recently had a
baby".

It was as a Wigan sixth form student that Anne-
Marie first came to terms with the figure in her art.
A founder member still working in the Artists in
Wigan Schools Scheme, she has, in turn, enabled
countless young people like Julie to discover that the
figure is likewise relevant to their needs and concerns. The support of the Director of Education and
Education Committee has been essential to the
Scheme growing and flourishing as it has done, due
mainly to the Director's convictions about the importance of these types of experiences to young
people's educational needs and the enrichment of
their lives.

9

Partnerships and Networks

"I think it lifted us out of a rut and gave us a much wider view of what children were supposed to be doing in school. The impetus still continues, 18 months later. There's an enthusiasm and a feeling that, well, we achieved that, so let's go on and try some more. It's taken some of the fear away from starting something new. We are now looking at the National Curriculum alongside the Wigan Entitlement, but at least we've got some idea now what the Wigan Entitlement is about, because this is a particular illustration of the Entitlement. The resistance to change has been reduced through a successful project."
Primary head teacher (1)

Many benefits to schools have already been highlighted. This head teacher testifies to the long-term effect of the changes as a result of a six-month placement by Andy Shaw. The changes he is talking about are basic to the school's whole thinking and philosophy. Elusive changes, because they are not going to be immediately apparent to the outsider who, having witnessed the residency, expects to see a recognisable legacy through the continued use of processes and materials, for example. Important changes, though, because head teacher and staff could address the demands of the National Curriculum by relating them to Wigan's extensive work over years with regard to an Entitlement Curriculum Policy. In the term prior to the introduction of the National Curriculum the residency had become the positive manifestation of so many facets of the Entitlement approach. The school was better placed to make sense of theory through practice in those initial National Curriculum deliberations.

Because of Andy's residency a group of second year junior pupils then visited the A-level student residencies at Winstanley College. The head teacher said,

"It had matured them in another way and now, in the third year, I think you can see a difference because they've had an experience which has meant something to them and, life is a series of experiences, isn't it!"

So, apart from more obvious legacies, the head teacher can trace positive attitudes in staff and pupils to the school's involvement in Wigan's residency schemes. In addition, of course, the concerns, concepts, processes and media introduced by artists modify and broaden what is on offer in clearly recognisable ways so that Kevin Hampson, Director of Education for Wigan, can say,

Junior pupils and sixth form students worked together on figure drawing from 4.00 to 6.00 pm at Winstanley College.

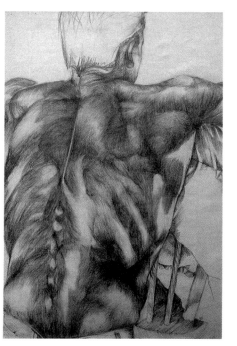

A study of the pose made by an A-level student.

Treatment of the same pose by an eight year-old: the scapula and vertebrae are clearly indicated, having been pointed out in the teacher's introduction to the session.

"As I walk around schools in Wigan, particularly schools which have had the presence of an artist-in-residence, then I do see things other than the crumpled coke can, the training shoe, etc. In other words, other than what I would call the basic examination-linked type of Art. We've seen it at Drumcroon with work from even very young children - much more developed art work, much more free-standing art work." (2)

However committed arts advisers and colleagues might be, what they can achieve is likely to be marginal without the direct support of the Director of Education or Chief Education Officer. Hampson and his predecessor, with whom he had worked very closely, subscribe to a philosophy of education in which the arts have a central role. The resources which have been built up centrally, allied to the partnership principle, ensure that thousands of young people and many schools benefit from the kinds of experiences to which the head teacher makes reference above. There has been a commitment to the provision of resources in terms of both quality and quantity. That these should build upon, but be over and above, what is on offer in any school is born out of the belief that,

"...of all the deprivations in this area - and most people look at social and economic deprivation, and particularly high unemployment levels - I've always argued strongly that the greatest deprivation is cultural, not just on the part of 'ordinary people' - as they perceive themselves - who one might expect to feel self-conscious in this respect, but on the part of better educated people who themselves have had better chances. My feeling is that all people should enjoy cultural experience, which in itself is to be supported but is also a means to greater creativity elsewhere and greater achievement."

Unfortunately, many of those who hold key posts in education were themselves denied access to the arts, having been educated in an era when the 'academically able' were assumed to have neither need nor time for arts experiences. Whereas many so educated, in their turn, undervalue the arts, Hampson wants all Wigan's young people to have the opportunities he was denied - it rankles with him that he cannot actively participate in them, through lack of educational opportunities at the key formative stage. He describes Drumcroon as the 'flagship' of the whole Wigan Arts Service, and believes the Artists in Wigan Schools Scheme to be one of its richest and key elements. His overview is therefore of great importance to this book, and the support of those in key posts is necessary for wider developments to be properly set up.

He cites Wigan's consistent achievement in external examinations as evidence of the wider ramifications of the philosophy. The Authority's place as 15th in the country, in terms of pupils gaining five or more high-graded GCSE or 16+ passes over three years, is particularly significant when it is considered that this takes no account of such factors as the local economy and environment. When these are considered, it becomes apparent that Wigan is performing way above its socio-economic standing. Hampson believes that this is a direct outcome of its high-profile arts policy and commitment, with the pupils' achievements being not just in the arts but across the curriculum for he has no doubt that there is

"...a direct correlation between an arts policy approach and external examination results because there is nothing else that is different about Wigan to explain those particular achievements. I put that down particularly to our wide Arts Entitlement helping to develop, more than anything else, confidence in pupils."

Though young Wiganers can be extremely confident with those they know, he feels that they can become introverted and fail to perform to the full in unfamiliar environments and in such circumstances as interviews.

"Now through the arts in the widest sense, pupils have been given the opportunities to recognise that they do have talents and that those talents have always been there. It's not purely for the highly intelligent, for many people have got multi-talents which they have never been allowed to develop. They have seen those talents develop now and that has given them a confidence which washes over everything else that they attempt. That sort of confidence, ultimately, has a direct effect on how they actually perform in standard, external examinations - but it's far more important in terms of how they develop as human beings!...The arts give pupils power by enabling them to communicate."

Personal and Social Education (PSE) is an issue which is currently under consideration and one could not have a more powerful statement about the significance of the arts. Yet, ironically, when PSE is timetabled - with all the inherent risks of contrivance - it is often at the expense of the arts subjects through which the issues can invariably be addressed.

Though the climate is hardly conducive to arts initiatives, the Director believes that in the interests of young people everywhere developments should be taking place. He emphasises that

"...there aren't any short cuts. You can't suddenly transcribe from Wigan into somewhere else the sort of system that we've spent years developing. You can transcribe some of the principles but you do have to ensure that you are following a basic movement of philosophy...a lot of people who come to Wigan, whilst they recognise what is being achieved on the artistic front, still regard the arts as peripheral and still worry that if they follow this sort of line something more important will go by the wayside. I think it is the basic philosophy that we have got to get over as quickly as possible, because individual government for individual schools will make the transference of that sort of philosophy more difficult than it has been in the past."

Though the Local Education Authority is undoubtedly the most effective agency through which to bring about the broadest change for the maximum number of young people in an area, the Education Reform Act and, in particular, Local Management of Schools (LMS) can militate against this. Hampson is far from pessimistic though,

"I think that partnership will be more important than ever. If partnership is not extended under

▲ On entering Tyldesley County Primary, the main corridor establishes the special ethos of a school in which the arts are central to its whole school policies.

Wigan's use of artists within an integrated visual arts service has had a dramatic impact on school environments: Tyldesley County Primary is an outstanding example.

Gilded Hollins primary pupils at work on a viking pot during Nikki Wilson's residency.

▲ A Tyldesley County Primary classroom display in which the colours, forms and textures were derived from those in the adjacently hung Schools Loan work by Paul Ryan.

Ian Murphy's work in 'Drumcroon: the First Ten Years'. As an A-level student he painted the Drumcroon porch (right), the work (centre) is from his 1985 degree show, the landscape (left) was completed in 1990.

The Turnpike Gallery artist-in-residence, 1985-86: Ian Murphy, born and educated in Wigan, has profoundly affected countless Wigan pupils through the Artists in Wigan Schools Scheme.

Ian Murphy's 1986-87 studio at Tyldesley County Primary then became a school-based art gallery named after him, as the sign outside the Murphy Room indicates.

The first Murphy Room exhibition: the pupil works seen here all derived from a week in the Lake District which Ian attended. The large paintings were for corridor displays, their irregular shapes being determined by stairs.

LMS then I can see nothing but a narrowing of the curriculum and limitation, which is the worry about testing...if governing bodies, head teachers or a combination went off doing their own thing, then while some of them might individually achieve some things of excellence and of great value, what was achieved would be piecemeal and nothing like as beneficial as if those individual pieces were put together."

Partnership between local authority and schools, with the former acting as supporter, "manipulator in some instances", but as facilitator more than anything else, is the best means of producing that "whole which is much, much greater than the individual parts".

"That will be lost if we don't establish, over the next two or three years, a complete understanding and belief in a Wigan Entitlement-style curriculum underpinned with its strong arts policy."

The alternative would be a more limited experience for pupils and, more critically and worrying, with the wider horizons which have been opened up for pupils being lost again. This would be worse than before in authorities like Wigan,

"...because we have seen what can be achieved through that broadening of experience, so to go back would feel to me like taking two big steps back and not just one."

Through partnership, then, such developments are not only still possible but are even more essential than hitherto because,

"If you look at the alternative, schools - because they lack that basic partnership - will tend to look at what will become national syllabuses to actually direct their teaching and, ultimately, their

teaching styles. Even if they attempt to resist it, they will be directly externally judged, so they will end up as in 11+ days teaching towards testing at 7, 11, 14 and 16. That will inevitably mean we will be back to that wonderful word 'basic' - whatever it means! But we know how it is interpreted - narrowly. And where does that leave the wider cultural experiences that the arts bring? I would go one step further and ask, 'Where does that leave us when we have evidence to prove that even those basic subjects narrowly interpreted are improved if you have a philosophy which actually enables children, in the widest sense possible, to experience the arts?'"

This is an even more pertinent issue now because, since the Director expressed those words, the Secretary of State has announced that standardised externally prescribed testing at 7, and probably at 11, will only be in the core subjects. Few would argue that, as originally envisaged, the National Curriculum placed an intolerable burden on teachers and pupils alike with its requirement that testing took place in all core and foundation subjects at 7, 11, 14 and 16. However, the clear evidence of 11+ days was that what was to be externally tested became what was taught. The dangers implicit in so testing only those subjects regarded as 'basic' are considerable: a system which constantly underlines the shortcomings of a good percentage of the school population would soon undermine the self-esteem and confidence of young people, whereas, as Hampson stresses, this self-esteem and confidence is one of the special contributions which a broad and imaginative arts policy has brought about in Wigan.

When unemployment and recession were at their height, and in the build up to the introduction of a National Curriculum, there were constant suggestions that education had been failing the nation - though, interestingly, there was no acclaim of its achievements when there was an upturn in the economy! It was customary to compare unfavourably what was happening here with the performances of certain other European countries. It was they and the North Americans, seemingly, who had the systems worthy of emulation. Interestingly, Hampson's visits to Angers in France, arising out of its twinning with Wigan, have provided him with a good basis from which to make comparisons.

"One of the things that bothered me about nationally laid down criteria for the curriculum was that in Europe central direction certainly affected the flexibility which was available. Indeed, in the week that we spent in Angers the

theme was that the towns twinned with Angers should compare their education systems. Angers is twinned not just with Wigan but with a Dutch town, an Italian town, a German town and one in Africa.

One of the things that came out of these comparisons was that in Wigan the artistic experience was much more practical, much more part of the environment, than anything that had ever been seen particularly by the French, but by the Europeans in general. In fact, they were saying to us, "Are those scenes, scenes in schools?" And we had to convince them that they were scenes in schools, and not untypical scenes in Wigan schools with artists-in-residence."

One particular incident - from one of Andy Shaw's residencies - aroused powerful responses when seen on video.

"The one outstanding effect on the European people was our 'Arts in Education' programme when they saw kids in the process of making huge animals, especially the one sitting on its back and slapping on plaster and fibreglass! That had an immediate impact - and we are not just talking about the officials representing the twinned towns, because this was also a public meeting. So the people of Angers were actually there, and were amazingly impressed at this and began to ask, 'Well, why can't we do this in French schools? Why can't our pupils have this sort of experience?'" (3)

The situation became rather embarrassing as the local officials were forced onto the defensive, but quite clearly the incident affirmed the Director's belief in the worth of Wigan's resources and in the Artists in Wigan Schools Scheme. Equally, it emphasised the importance of Drumcroon as the base and support ensuring that the artists are not thrown entirely onto their own resources.

Though visitors frequently use the word 'unique' in reference to Drumcroon, the concept certainly need not remain so. This country contains an abundance of potential venues and under-used resources which could be revitalised through a long-term education commitment based on partnership principles. Many galleries and museums could benefit through the process.

"Drumcroon has provided a special focus which could be developed anywhere given a positive approach to providing artistic experience. If people are positive and feel that they can achieve

development via the arts, then they will actually achieve it. They can provide that focus wherever and at whatever level..."

Rooted as it is within the education system, Drumcroon is staffed and administered by personnel with extensive school experience and who therefore naturally 'speak the same language' as teachers. It highlights how Wigan has pioneered imaginative developments by giving particular individuals the freedom and licence to make use of their special gifts and flair, and to nurture and develop such projects to maturity. In the process, a team of like-thinking people has been formed.

"There has got to be a fair level of commitment at the heart. You cannot do radical things in half measures, you do have to create space for people...if you create space for the right sort of people, you create space for them to become creative, for them to actually affect philosophies and environments. Amazingly enough, having created space for them the experience is that they then more than fill the space!...you get repaid tenfold for the small amount of space you create for a central group of people...we would then hope, obviously, that that would create another set of people who would learn from, and pick up enthusiasm from, the original core."

At any given time there are relatively few people with the capacity to innovate, so wherever they are to be found they must make up the 'original core' - even though monitoring and inspectoral duties envisaged for advisers may shift the emphasis more to advisory support staff in the future. The dedicated team which has grown out of this process ensures that Drumcroon, the Turnpike Gallery, the Wigan Schools Loan Collection and the Artists in Wigan Schools Scheme function effectively as an integrated Service. The wealth of support material which they produce to tight deadlines ensures that what is on offer has become embedded in the work of many schools' practice and is continuing to be used.

The use particularly of local artists has also facilitated their integration into this Service. Prior to Drumcroon, all this 'local talent' was lost to Wigan, unless a former student returned as a teacher. Their positive role in Wigan is a logical extension of Hampson's argument that the arts provide a vehicle for opening up to the pupils an awareness of their own multi-talents.

"If they are from the same communities as the pupils, then one of the great advantages is that the artists recognise themselves in those kids. In other words, they can see how they used to be through the kids and I think that relationship actually enables the artists to give more to those pupils, to understand that lack of confidence in them and to develop it through the practical use and development of their talents. Ultimately it's a two-way process, isn't it? What the kids themselves then bring first-hand to those experiences actually helps the artist to further develop his or her individual talent and confidence - not just in dealing with kids but in dealing with the extension of what might be interpreted as their own artistic experiences."

The regional arts associations have done much of the pioneering work in getting artists working in schools recognised, and Wigan has benefited greatly from its close working relationship with North West Arts. Nevertheless, having and believing in an Entitlement Curriculum Policy demands that the concept is advanced much further to take account of the needs of all young people. By what criteria should an artist work in one school as opposed to all the others in a locality? By what criteria is a particular 'target group' selected within a school in preference to all the other pupils? Insufficient artists available allied to inadequate funding are traditionally why these kinds of arbitrary decisions have had to be made. Yet most communities possess a similar reservoir of local artistic talent ready and willing to be creatively harnessed; the implications are considerable!

"So that all schools can ultimately have this sort of experience, I argue strongly that this is exactly why you need local artists in local communities in link terms. To link directly with the kids and then in themselves to provide that link to more experienced artists and eventually right through to famous artists, whether at a direct and personal level or via the works of those individuals at any particular phase. That seems to me to be the basis for ultimately flooding the educational system by using every resource that is actually available. In particular, by using the resource of local people to produce waves of young people who can produce art of a particularly high quality to bridge the gap between the handful of outstanding practitioners right back to the kid in school."

The Artists in Wigan Schools Scheme inevitably began to attract artists from beyond the Local Authority boundaries, but the strong nucleus of locally educated young artists are potent daily reminders of Hampson's belief in promoting a service which seeks to develop those multi-talents in Wigan's young people. What better form of employment than that they, in turn, go on to develop the skills of the next generation!

Another major by-product of Hampson's belief in ultimately flooding the educational system in relation to Entitlement needs is cross-fertilisation of experiences for schools. Wigan's residencies have generated tremendous interest amongst teachers to the point where it has become perfectly natural for those in one school to visit another to see developments in a residency. This has led to an important form of networking through which schools are thinking about the natural implications of a residency in advance of one taking place. Similarly, the problems inherent in an artist going into a school 'cold' are dramatically reduced, for many opportunities exist, through Drumcroon and Turnpike previews and meetings, a whole variety of in-service situations for artists to get to know teachers. Reports on residencies around the country reveal evidence of the same or similar problems and misunderstandings recurring over and over again, and they will doubtless continue to do so in the absence of

a) a central support and contact base for artists such as is provided in Wigan by the Drumcroon Education Art Centre;

b) strategies aimed at identifying artists and aiding them to develop skills relating to communication as well as practice;

c) coherent policies and programmes designed to create networks and clusters of schools hosting artists, as opposed to individual artists undertaking residencies on a one-off basis by whatever criteria;

d) setting-up residencies within the contexts of overall authority policies on the one hand, and whole school policies on the other.

It is through 'networking' conceived around such criteria that schools, artists and organising and support agencies can begin to build upon and benefit from the experiences gained in other residencies so that maximum systematic use is made of the artists working within the area.

The Calouste Gulbenkian Foundation commissioned this book with a view to it spreading the principles and the nature of the work undertaken in Wigan. Both Drumcroon and the Artists in Wigan Schools Scheme have, in recent years, attracted many visitors, some from far afield. The perspectives and experience which have been brought into Wigan through such visitors have had a regenerative effect on what has been taking place and, in turn, many

have returned home nurturing ambitions for related initiatives in their areas. Some of these now exist, in whole or in part, or are in the process of realisation. If the support of the Director of Education is of paramount importance, so the creative spark of the initiator is also absolutely essential. From the many resulting projects which have arisen, therefore, the concluding section of this book is devoted to a handful which indicate something of the wide range of possibilities open to those capable of making the imaginative leap from the philosophy and principles to particular situations and contexts.

A number of school galleries - mini-Drumcroons - have now been established: the inaugral Hawkley Gallery exhibition was of work by Ken Cottam.

Two members of the Artists in Wigan Schools Scheme, Norma Tait and Sue Peterson, provided the second Hawkley Gallery exhibition.

10

Wider Developments

"The most excitement for me was gained through the observation of the children's art that came from their workshop experiences with the artists. This work revealed an enrichment which goes beyond just acknowledging adult art through observation. At Wigan they experienced a total immersion into the wonder of Art...Here you have an entire community involved in the Arts, ie Children through Artists, Artists through Children, Parents through Children to Artists, Artists to Parents through Children, etc...Sure this has occurred in isolated spots in New Zealand, but not in the concentrated way as in Wigan." (1)

Visual arts developments, particularly those involving artists-in-residence, have attracted a steady stream of visitors to Wigan in recent years. These have led to many initiatives taking place not only in this country but around the world. Through his visit to Wigan, the Auckland College lecturer quoted above became a confirmed critical studies enthusiast. His previous scepticism, born out of reservations about young people being stuffed full of facts and data about art on the one hand and of them 'apeing Cézanne' by copying reproductions on the other, was swept aside. The extract is from correspondence between him and the Curricular Officer for Art in the New Zealand Department of Education. In its wisdom, the New Zealand government has since seen fit to abolish the Department of Education, taking greater power to itself in the name of giving it to parents and governors. However, in the period leading to abolition, the Curricular Officer was able to report that, "Some teachers have since carried out useful artist-in-schools projects in their own area, especially as they see how well it relates to the thrust of the new Art syllabus." He describes one particular residency which "was inspired directly" by Wigan material to the extent that the teacher, "borrowed my copy of your book *Educating for Art* until he received his own copy". In all probability, though, an agency such as the Department of Education is sorely needed for further developments there on other than a piecemeal and fragmentary basis! (2)

Considerable commitment is also evidenced by the Senior Education Officer at the Western Australian Art Gallery in Perth following his visit to Wigan during which he, too, was able to witness a number of residencies,

"The excitement I felt at witnessing the Drumcroon experiment has not diminished one jot in a month and thousands of miles removed. For

A Raku Works residency, involving two ceramicists, gave rise to the magnificent Ceramic Fantasy Village at St Andrew's Primary School. Situated in the school entrance area, it elicts many responses and is a source of pride, every pupil having contributed to its making.

me it really was an illuminating experience...I shall be doing all that I can to spread the message of your philosophy and practice to art educators here in Western Australia and, in a more diluted form, I'm afraid, to my colleagues in other Australian public galleries...1987 will see the adaptation of some of your Drumcroon practices to the programme...at this Gallery." (3)

The head of the Art department at one of Archbishop Desmond Tutu's non-racial schools in Cape Town spent a week in Wigan on study research and writes,

"I returned to South Africa full of enthusiasm and inspiration. I am happy to say that my headmaster agreed to a trial artist-in-residence programme for 1990. Our first resident was a ceramicist, Katherine Glenday, and her superb porcelain work drew much positive response. During the second quarter of the year we will host a printmaker and sculptor, Viyile Vuyiya...I look back with great fondness to the time I spent in Wigan and the real privilege it was to share in what you are doing there...when I left Wigan I had no idea that less than a year later the dramatic events of recent weeks would have taken place. With Nelson Mandela's release from prison, the possibility of deliverance from the tragedy of apartheid rule seems tantalizingly close." (4)

In his resulting report, *The Critical Studies in Art Education Project: its significance and value for South African Educators,* he naturally emphasises the Wigan strategies designed to meet multicultural needs, but also records,

"During my stay at Drumcroon, and during various visits to schools in the area, I was struck by the vital impact that many of the resident artists had made in their respective schools...A memorable residency I observed was that of the artist Andy Shaw...The greatest treat was in store when I stepped into the art area to view the most extraordinary flowering of creative talent. Through exposure to Shaw's animal themes and working processes, the children had been spurred on to produce drawings and large animal

sculptures. There was, however, no hint of a mere pastiche of Shaw's sculpture in the children's work...If anything, the most obvious influence was that of the children's art on Andy Shaw's own work!" (5)

Referred to in the chapter on Shaw, some of the pupil's work is designed for display on a station and the report has a section 'Art on View' in which the author says that

"The single most important lesson I learned from my visit to Wigan was the importance of exposing art and craft objects to the school community in a way which would stimulate interest and inform the uninitiated...One of the most impressive examples I saw of child art displayed for the benefit and pleasure of the community was the 'Four Seasons' murals... permanently displayed at the Wigan Children's Library. The history of this work and the teaching involved reads like a master plan for successful Art teaching."

Of the many widespread influences of the Artists in Wigan Schools Scheme, it is particularly gratifying that a teacher in a South African non-racial school is bringing such powerful influences to bear on his own practice through a residency programme, and wider dissemination, at the present time in that country's history!

A similar week was undertaken by an Art teacher from a Service Children's School in Germany. In his report he records that "It has provided me with the experience of seeing how an initiative is interpreted and used in schools and has left me with a wealth of information and ideas", though it also led to self-analysis,

"My approach to teaching art has been shallow, offering only aspects from within my own areas of experience. This has created predictable responses from pupils and I hope by increasing the use of influence by other artists and art works I can broaden the nature of my teaching and provide a more meaningful and exciting programme." (6)

He will make better use of slide material immediately and "in the near future a programme of gallery visits needs to be arranged" but,

"It would be highly desirable to give the initiative impetus by having an artist-in-residence. The idea has been welcomed by the school but funding for the event has to be discussed at a future School Amenities Meeting. I feel confident that an artist involved in the Artists in Wigan Schools Scheme would be ideal for an initial residency."

The school agreed to fund a fortnight-long residency, and Anne-Marie Cadman, being self-employed, proved an ideal artist. Other Services Schools in Northern Germany are naturally looking with interest at this residency. They experience special problems of isolation and feel that resources like artists - given language problems, etc - are out of their reach.

Coming nearer to home, the art adviser for Barnet was stimulated to find funding for an art critic/historian following his visit to Drumcroon's second Artists in Wigan Schools exhibition - one, however, "who must not be an ivory tower intellectual but...who can unlock doors for our pupils, regardless of ability". (7) Dr Anabel Thomas was appointed, and at an early stage in her residency a teacher felt able to write,

"A few months ago I would never have thought I could sit on the floor of the Royal Academy with a bunch of lively third years and get them to tell me about Henry Moore, with all the rather posh tourists and art afficionados listening in amusement! (This happened on a visit which Anabel couldn't join - I was terrified, but it was great.)"

Such had been her impact, affirmed by the head of department's acknowledgement that "Dr Thomas has introduced a rich variety of visual and intellectual stimulus, new artists, new ideas backed by a relevant body of collected resource material."

The resource of the art historian - relatively plentiful in the area - is central to a Cambridgeshire project aimed at monitoring around 250 young people over a five year period. The Assistant Director of the project aims to build on the Wigan Scheme, following her visit, by using artists who will communicate about how they became artists, their training, etc, as well as making art, for they will operate in tandem with the art historians involved.

"The overall aim of this programme is to link the three areas central to art education, critical

appreciation of the cultural domain, participation, and critical self-evaluation...Classrooms and museum-based activities will combine to provide the basis on which assessment can take place of the pupils' acquisitions of the skills necessary to the making of informed aesthetic judgements." (8)

Of the various groups who visit Wigan, it is customary for numerous PGCE courses to pay annual visits. An item in the Leigh *Journal*,

"Local schools are among the forerunners in art education and have gained an enviable reputation nationally. On Tuesday a party of postgraduate art teachers visited Tyldesley and Leigh...Cardiff's principal art education lecturer praised the high standard of art education within the borough. 'The area's reputation as a leader in this field is nationally known.'" (9)

His South Glamorgan Institute students maintained a demanding schedule; following an overnight stay, Drumcroon was the first stop, then three school visits, concluding with an evening session at the Turnpike Gallery. These visits, combined with reciprocal ones to Cardiff, gave rise to the Institute's own innovative variant utilising the special "artistic strengths" of the "BA Art and Design specialisms" of the students. In place of the traditional primary school observation days, at an early stage of the course the students grouped into small teams designed to "demonstrate a range of Art and Design experience and expertise to young pupils". They set up studio areas in 14 schools, each of which enjoyed "45 cumulative artists-in-residence days". The college fully documented and evaluated the project with a view to wider dissemination.

"The self-confidence gained by working from the individual's strength and discipline provided a secure base from which exploratory and often adventurous work was carried out...Because it was a social context it encouraged the artists-in-residence to reflect upon the directions of the work, re-kindle and develop ideas and presented a new perspective upon the relevance of the work to others, including children...It was almost a natural way into teaching with the advantage that it emerged rather than being pre-conceived. Teaching was presented not as 'token giving' but as engaging in discussion and providing opportunities to explore any particular concern." (10)

Significantly, the report also noted that,

The giant horse of Standish High School, built in a courtyard and based on the Indian temple horses, was another ambitious Raku Works project: while drying out prior to firing, it provided unusual drawing stimulus: the wood firing, spanning a three-day period, was spectacular at night.

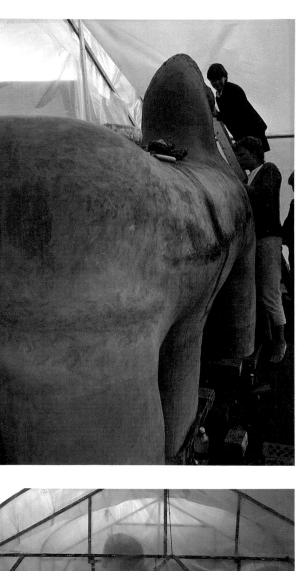

"...as the project developed, the priorities for many of the artists-in-residence moved to the work of the children. The pupils' enthusiasm and ability to initiate ideas became adventurous directions which could be followed through because of the small numbers involved. 'The problems had more to do with disappointing them, than with finding ways of interesting them.'"

These workshops "helped many artists-in-residence to attempt a range of projects and different methods of working that they would not have considered under student/teacher conditions". The invaluable wedding of special practical skills to those of communication makes an ideal beginning to the teacher training year, and is in marked contrast to those Art and Design teachers who feel that the teacher training year artificially severed their hard-gained specialist skills from the job of teaching. The Cardiff model, by contrast, is in keeping with Peter Abbs' assertion that,

"...something like an apprenticeship model of artistic learning is called for. The teacher enters as co-artist possessing, where necessary, clear lines of access to the aesthetic field. Following this model, the teacher of an arts discipline becomes, in some measure, a practitioner: the music teacher composes; the teacher of literature writes and edits; the teacher of dance dances; and each should be ready, at times, to act as creative exemplar." (11)

One of the primary head teachers involved in the project conjectures, "Could it be that multi-disciplinary workshops from across the disciplines, in Teacher Training, will evolve from such schemes?" An exhibition of the residencies is currently touring other PGCE centres and has, in turn, generated further related initiatives and variants.

The Artists in Wigan Schools Scheme, utilising the skills of young artists many of whom themselves were educated in Wigan, provides evidence of the significance of formative experiences at the school stage: those who themselves were affected by illuminating experiences seem to have an increased capacity to engender them in others. In turn, this indicates the importance of what might take place at the BA Honours phase of education.

Geoff Brunell's Drumcroon 'Joie de Vivre' exhibition provided the focus for the Fine Print students from Manchester to work in Wigan schools. On his move to the Polytechnic of East London he has since developed the concept to the point where second year undergraduates of sculpture, painting and print have undertaken residencies in schools and colleges in four neighbouring boroughs. Their importance to

Only £30 had been added to the Art department's capitation in support, but the impact had been such that, as a follow-up, the school plans to have "a Sculptress-in-Residence and I have every confidence that her contribution will be as valuable as the previous two artists".

The Polytechnic's course outline describes the residency scheme as "similar in structure to the one pioneered by...Wigan," and with each placement lasting between four and six weeks and for five days per week. Wigan principles are clearly to the fore,

Two art forms gave added meaning to each other when Philip Smith's drama studio mural, executed during rehearsals, was complemented by pupils performing The Quadrangle by Beckett: view of mural and audience.

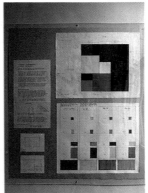

Supporting information, displayed alongside Philip Smith's mural, made the mathematical principles clear.

The principles governing Philip Smith's work led to a painted mural at the entrance to the mathematics suite during his Hesketh Fletcher High School residency.

the host institutions as well as the students is reflected in the response of a head teacher who recorded that Andrea and Yvonne

"...joined us in an innovative educational venture where they were involved with teachers and students interweaving their artistic skills into the curricula of this school. Pupils were allowed to practise their art skills, critically evaluate each other's work and their own, and analyse what it was they were doing, why they were doing it and what would be the outcome.

The level of activity, sustained attention and sense of discovery, surpassed anything our young students (11-14 years) had ever done before...I have never seen so much colour and large canvasses around the school. Pupils brought in artefacts, many reflecting their ethnic and cultural backgrounds. They observed other girls dancing and moving and the anatomical structure of the human body as well as observing body movement and then drawing the movement lines..." (12)

"The underlying structure is that the student (as the artist) spends 50% of his/her time practising as an artist in a space provided by the institution, and 50% of the time working in collaboration with the teaching staff on projects negotiated between the artist and the teacher with the pupils...The residencies are supported by an exhibition of the artist's work mounted within the school." (13)

Brunell's working relationship with Drumcroon had been that of like-thinking minds coming together, with one of his major concerns being that students should develop communication skills through interactive social situations as an essential part of their studies. With this in mind - after an introduction to the school - "artists are left to discuss the nature of the residency directly with the staff," but with care taken over choice of schools "as there is little point in exposing students to negative environments".

To better help pupils understand their work, the students place it within an art historical context through use of slides, initially tested out on their peers in half-day a week seminars in support of the residencies. Some of these presentations are "outstanding", with intriguing autobiographical and anecdotal information. They help "bond the students and increase the group awareness" as well as acting as "sounding boards as all students have problems they need to air". Some students experience a sense of achievement through these projects which has "taken many of the staff by surprise".

"To work independently, to have had a work experience, gives them a great sense of accomplishment, increases their self-awareness and self-confidence. Also the analysis of children's working processes stimulates their imagination, liberates and qualifies their own work and the course teaching."

There are polytechnic lecturers with reservations about such projects arguing that they erode time from the real coursework, but Brunell maintains that

"There is no way that the residency scheme can be seen as a dilution of the student's Fine Art experience. For many it is the most intense experience of their lives and is a qualification of what they have learnt so far, often transforming their approach in the studio on their return."

New levels of motivation frequently lead to heightened studio activity and output on the return to college and the scheme has, in turn, spawned another vital model - that of young artists undertaking short-term residencies within the polytechnic. One of these, Anthony Lysycia, is a former Wigan student and has exhibited and been in residence at Drumcroon also in company with his carved doors, chests and barrels, prints, stone carvings and paintings - further emphasising the links between the two schemes.

This experiment involving BA Honours students hints at the vast reservoir of talent which can be harnessed in mutually beneficial ways; in addition to Fine Art students, there are those studying in the fields of architecture; graphics and computer technology, fashion and textiles, product, interior and theatre design and a range of three-dimensional activities. The potential for them to provide young people with added insights into the breadth of the art, design and technology spectrum is immense. The students' own career possibilities can likewise be broadened with those who choose to go into teaching or into community work choosing from greater knowledge and awareness.

Combine the North East London and Cardiff models and it is immediately apparent that, across the country, thousands of young people and students

alike could benefit through interactions and insights.

Polytechnic course leaders are the obvious organisers of such student projects, but their partnership with local authority personnel is essential if the need to provide concentrated coverage within areas and communities is to be met. A Staff Development and Support Teacher in a West Midlands authority, comparable to Wigan in size and nature, is one who is eager to take on this task. His initial Wigan visit was followed by another in the company of 14 teachers. As well as thereby arousing interest and support, they have also contributed to the process of identifying the range of possibilities relevant to the needs of their authority. The Support Teacher writes

"As a follow-up to our visit I had arranged for a one-day INSET with all of the teachers who attended. The aim of the day was to lay down some guidelines as to what we in Sandwell could sensibly aim at. As a result of this meeting we intend to invite all teachers of Art and Design (including textiles teachers and teachers in special schools) to an open session where we put to them the ideas formed during the day: ideas such as 1) Greater integration/liaison with our own Art Gallery/Museum 2) Possible secondment of teacher(s) to act as artists in schools 3) Your idea of Government Enterprise grants being used with artists to work in schools 4) The possibility of establishing our own educational gallery (not, I hasten to add, on the same scale as your own!) 5) A Sandwell Schools Loan Collection to include original artworks/artefacts, slides, videos, books, good quality reproductions 6) Tapping external sources of revenue 7) Liaising with Colleges of Education to enlist PGCE students as artists-in-schools 8) The establishing of our own Art and Design newsletter." (14),

He adds,

"The enthusiasm amongst those teachers who visited your gallery is tremendous. I just hope that I can channel it into positive corporate action that will lead to greater enrichment of experience offered to our children within the whole sphere of 'Art'."

Numerous administrative hurdles will doubtless have to be cleared but the collective will and the commitment of a motivated individual should ensure that something of worth is achieved. The objectives defined represent a goal not too dissimilar to that identified in Wigan at a time when resources were at a premium. Resident artists, whether teachers, students or professional practitioners, are all part of the concept and will doubtless find support within such a scheme. That such broad-based aims need to develop over a realistic timespan has already been highlighted!

Many other examples of groups and individuals attempting similar developments within their localities could be cited, they all highlight that

1) The individual teacher can successfully argue the case to obtain school funding for the short-term residency.

Note: A consortia approach involving a number of schools in an area might be the best means of obviating piecemeal achievement at a time when the Poll Tax and Local Management of Schools might be inhibiting at the local authority level.

2) The gallery can develop residency schemes to benefit the schools within the vicinity.

3) PGCE students can participate in residency schemes which can be of benefit to them and the schools involved.

4) Undergraduate students can likewise benefit while offering invaluable benefit to schools (similarly those on MA courses).

5) Local authority personnel remain the most vital agencies for the establishment and running of coherent schemes designed to address the Entitlement needs of all young people within a community.

The first point relates to the one-off residency whereas the main thrust of this book is about the Entitlement needs of all pupils. However, that is where the individual teacher has to begin, and such residencies often provide the catalyst for further developments. In activities like the 'Print Extravaganza', described by Marina Vaizey, the skills of students, teacher-artists, exhibiting and established artists are all simultaneously harnessed to effect, but each category can make its particular contributions, when properly co-ordinated, over a period of time.

To conclude, then, all these agencies are used when appropriate under the umbrella of the Artists in Wigan Schools Scheme with the interests and needs of all young people in mind, in keeping - particularly - with the third Wigan Principle:

"3. Education must respond equally to the needs of all individuals. The needs of individual people may be different but any one need is of no greater importance than any other." (15)

In its realisation, all the other Principles can be demonstrated to have been addressed in significant ways, for wide-ranging thinking has to be rigorously applied if the needs of all young people are indeed going to be adequately met.

The underlying philosophy has enabled people with differing talents to work together to their mutual benefit but, ultimately, for the greater benefit of vast numbers of young people. Through their exposure to the Artists in Wigan Schools Scheme, many have demonstrated clear evidence of being affected in heightened ways about art and through exceptional practical achievement. In the process, arguments about artists being funded at the expense of children's better interests; of artists being able to do what teachers are therefore assumed to be unable to do; of the proper place for artists being in private studios etc, pale into insignificance. The testimonies throughout this book make clear that, given a sound philosophical base and support, wider community, teacher, artist and child can all benefit through their shared involvement based upon clearly-defined educational goals.

The most successful artists share a number of important characteristics; these are worth bearing in mind when similar schemes are being formulated and suitable artists identified.

1) Each of these artists is individual in the skills and approaches he or she brings to the job. They are able to work from their special distinctive strengths, secure in the knowledge that these provide the necessary basis for their work in schools.

2) Nevertheless, these artists are sufficiently versatile to be able to connect their skills, in co-operation with teachers, to school courses, themes, projects, topics, etc.

3) They are capable of developing their work naturally and without contrivance while working in a public place, in spite of all the pressures this inevitably involves.

4) They are willing and able communicators who give thought to how they might effectively express themselves in words as well as through their artistic practice. They can operate with young people of differing ages, abilities and aptitudes as well as with adults.

5) They are willing and able to work in close co-operation and partnership with teachers on a giving and sharing basis.

6) They are able to create visual impact from when they first enter a school through the attractive and informative ways in which they present their work and contextualise it.

7) Besides the obvious interest which they generate

(Far left) Geoff Brunell's 'Joie de Vivre' Drumcroon exhibition and the Wigan 'Print Extravanganza' influenced his student residency schemes at the Polytechnic of East London.

Two pupils working in the Drumcroon Main Gallery during 'Joie de Vivre'.

Peter Oakley, a college lecturer studying on the Fine Print MA course at the time of 'Joie de Vivre', taking a print while in residency at Drumcroon.

Anthony Lysycia, in residence at Drumcroon, provides a further link with the Polytechnic of East London, having also been in residence there.

through their own work, they also effectively involve young people in the study of other related artists, past and present.

8) Working within an authority-wide service with its support structures, they are able to make their impact felt on a broader basis than just within the school in which they are resident.

It has been demonstrated that even students at the A-level stage can have abilities allied to communication skills, worth sharing with other young people. They speak the same language as these younger 'Wiganers' as, of course, do the recently graduated artists from the same community and those who have closely identified with it. Unlike the Lion-in-Residence in 'A Parable', working in schools has, in fact, removed the invisible bars which had been effectively caging them when they were working alone without support, materials, facilities, sustainable ambition or motivation, or contact with like-thinking people.

How many other artists with commensurate skills are there hidden away throughout the country? How many young lives might they enrich, inform and benefit if afforded the appropriate opportunities? How many other interested parties are there in appropriate posts and with the necessary energy and vision to harness these young artists' skills and to provide the support systems capable of cultivating and developing them? There is still much that needs to be done in Wigan to meet the needs of all young people in these respects. Marina Vaizey highlights the need for wider application of the principles,

"While the Drumcroon-Wigan model has yet to be copied nationally, every time there is a workshop at an art gallery, or an artist in a school now, something of what has happened at Drumcroon this past decade is reflected. If the message were carried on, eventually many of us, or our children, could at last be visually alert, so attuned that the ghastly mess we make of our environment would be altered. This is what art-in-education should be about: not only doing, but thinking." (16)

Anthony Lysycia's ambitious carved doors and prints in Drumcroon during his one-person 'Lifelines' exhibition. The two left hand works are now in the Wigan School Loans Collection and are in constant demand.

Postscript

Between completion of the above manuscript and its publication, Metropolitan Wigan was 'Poll Capped' by the government following the introduction of the Poll Tax. Amongst the adversely affected services, the following are directly relevant to this text:

* The Artists in Wigan Schools Scheme salary bill was halved. Seven artists accepted employment on a half-time basis with only four retained full-time. Four left the Scheme, including Kevin Johnson, who features prominently in these pages; he obtained a full-time teaching post in another authority.
* The Drumcroon Gallery Education Officer applied for, and was appointed to, a teacher training post in higher education. He cannot be replaced.
* The services of the Assistant Gallery Education Officer had to be dispensed with because she was on a temporary post. She cannot be replaced.
* Drumcroon's exhibition programme has been reduced from six shows a year to four as a cost-cutting measure.
* The Schools Loan Officer was on a temporary post. Her salary, covering a twelve-month period, has been successfully obtained through the support of two independent foundations.
* The purchase of all library books, etc and Schools Loan works has ceased; demand for works currently exceeds what is available.
* It was not possible to second a teacher to work as Drumcroon artist-in-residence for 1990-91, breaking a sequence of ten such artists extending back to 1980.

Amongst the personnel who remain, the commitment to maintain the quality of service established is undiminished, though it has to be accepted that it is no longer realistic to attempt to address the Entitlement needs of all the Wigan young people engaged in full-time education to the degree that these have been pursued. The support of teachers for the service on offer has been overwhelming, with many anxious to find ways of maintaining it. It has been necessary to further reduce the school-based residencies by artists within the Scheme, for the skills of some are having to be harnessed to maintain the Drumcroon service.

Though the service has been seriously impaired, its underlying principles are well tried, proved to be effective, and beneficial to the educational, personal and social needs of children and young people of all ages and abilities. The current climate is detrimental to creative enterprises of an educational nature, but the guiding principles upon which the Drumcroon service and Artists in Wigan Schools Scheme have been founded will doubtless stand in good stead others engaged in similar future initiatives. Hopefully, this book will help inform and stimulate some such ventures.

References

Introduction

1. *Red Book 3: The Wigan Chapter* (DES 11-16 Curriculum Project) Wigan LEA, 1984.

2. Braden, Su. *Artists and People,* Routledge & Kegan Paul, 1978.

3. Smith, Ralph A (editor). *Artists-in-Schools: Analysis and Criticism,* Bureau of Educational Research, University of Illinois, 1978.

1 Drumcroon

1. Dyson, Anthony. 'Art and Design: A Parting of Ways', *Curriculum Progress 5-16: School Subjects and the National Curriculum Debate* (editors Patrick Wiegand and Michael Raynor), the Falmer Press, 1989.

2. 'Introducing Art to the Community: How the Drumcroon Education Art Centre in Wigan was set up', *Broadsheet 23,* DES Architects and Building Branch, June 1987.

3. Vaizey, Marina. 'How 51 artists are teaching Wigan a lesson', *The Sunday Times,* 17 May 1987.

4. 'Treescapes' catalogue, Drumcroon, June 1988.

5. 'Artists in Wigan Schools' catalogue, Drumcroon, September 1985.

6. Extract from student's A-level 'mock' examination paper, 1989.

7. 'Michael Rothenstein' catalogue, jointly published by Angela Flowers, Drumcroon, and Turnpike Galleries, November 1988, covering three exhibitions between November 1988 and March 1989.

8. '3' catalogue, Drumcroon, June 1983.

9. Letter to Drumcroon from pupil, 1983.

10. 'Fragments' catalogue, Drumcroon, June 1989.

11. From pupils written work (used for GCSE English examination), 1989.

12. Primary deputy head teacher's documentation of school's use of Amanda Faulkner exhibition and residency of Anne-Marie Quinn in relation to 'My Body' project (Tyldesley County Primary School).

2 The Artists in Wigan Schools: Beginnings

1. 'Artists in Wigan Schools' catalogue (op cit), statement by Gillian Travers.

2. Application to MSC, 'Artists in Schools Proposal', Wigan, June 1984.

3. Vaizey, Marina. 'The art of winning prizes', *The Sunday Times,* 3 November 1985.

4. 'Artists in Wigan Schools' catalogue (op cit).

5. Residency evaluation, Head of Art, Golborne Comprehensive, September 1985.

6. Residency evaluation, Head of Art, Abraham Guest High School, September 1985.

7. Residency evalution, Head of Art, Cardinal Newman High School, September 1985.

8. From recorded interview with Keith Walker, Summer Term 1986. Extracts are included throughout the chapter. (Keith Walker was on secondment as Manchester Polytechnic PGCE lecturer at time of interview, returning to school post in the September. He was appointed to post of Drumcroon Gallery Education Officer in January 1988, where he worked until returning to Manchester Polytechnic as PGCE lecturer in September 1990.)

9. Eram is depicted wearing this dress on the cover and inside the CSAE book *Educating for Art* (Longman, 1986); there are also 3 plates of her wearing clothes of European and Asian design which she made as a 'Home Art' interest.

3 Intimate Relationships

1. Pupil's writing incorporated into art work: 'My Body' project.

2. Entry in residency diary kept by artist.

3. Residency diary (op cit).

4. From recorded interview with Dave Burton and Pat Basano, July 1986. Extracts are included throughout 'A Children's Art Treasure Hunt' section of chapter.

5. Residency evaluation in letter form, dated 27 February 1986, to author by head teacher. The following pupil statements are incorporated into this letter.

6. From research into art, craft and design in the Wigan primary sector conducted by Advisory Teacher for Art (Primary), unpublished.

7. From recorded interview with the artist. Extracts are included throughout the chapter.

8. Taylor, Brandon. 'Art History in the Classroom: a plea for caution', *Critical Studies in Art and Design Education* (editor David Thistlewood), Longman & NSEAD, 1989.

9. Written statement by pupil: 'My Body' project.

4 George Orwell and Children's Art for Public Places

1. Vistors' book entries, Andy Shaw residency exhibition, April 1989.

2. Pupil writing on display, residency exhibition.

3. Pupil writing on display, residency exhibition.

4. From recorded interview with the artist, April 1989. Extracts are included throughout the chapter.

5. From recorded interview with head teacher, Nicol Mere

Primary School, 1989.

6. From recorded interviews with pupils conducted by the author in the school during the week of residency exhibition.

7. Front page, *Wigan Evening Post,* Saturday 14 May 1988.

8. Interview with head teacher (op cit).

9. Letter addressed to Wigan Director of Education, dated 12 April 1989.

5 Special Needs and a Special Approach to Ceramics

1. From a recorded interview with the Head of Art, Standish Mere Oaks Special School, March 1989. Extracts are included throughout the chapter.

2. From a recorded interview with the artist, March 1989. Extracts are included throughout the chapter.

6 'On Being a Black Artist in Britain'

1. Samuels, Joan. Letter to the author, dated 28 January 1987.

2. *Red Book 3: The Wigan Chapter* (op cit).

3. Teacher evaluations of Wigan INSET residential course, February/March 1989.

4. Taylor, Rod. 'Anti-racism and Multicultural-ism in the Visual Arts' paper. NB: the aims quoted have since been

incorporated in the Wigan Arts Policy document, 'A Policy Statement', published in 1990.

5. Teacher residential course evaluation (op cit).

6. From a recorded interview with the artist, May 1989. Extracts are included throughout the chapter.

7. From a report by Roger Stanley, teacher at the Gloucester School, West Germany, following his research study week in Wigan, April 1989.

8. Written responses by students to presentation by artist at Winstanley Sixth Form College, March 1989.

9. Roger Stanley report (op cit).

10. From a recorded interview with the pupil, May 1989.

7 The Enterprise Board Artists

1. From a recorded interview with the artist, January 1989. Extracts are included throughout the chapter.

2. 'Connections' cata-logue, Drumcroon, September 1988.

3. From a recorded interview with the head teacher, Atherton Hindsford Primary School, June 1989.

4. From a recorded interview with the deputy head teacher, June 1989.

8 Sixth Form College Pioneering Initiatives

1. Student's written Personal Appraisal statement, October 1986.

2. From recorded interviews with students conducted by Head of Art, Spring 1987 (Wigan Arts in Schools Project research).

3. From a recorded interview with College Principal, 1986 (Arts in Schools research).

4. From a recorded interview conducted by Head of Art, Spring 1987 (Arts in Schools re-search). Extracts are included throughout the chapter.

5. Student interviews (see 2 above).

6. From a recorded interview with the teacher by the Head of Art, 1987 (Arts in Schools re-search).

7. Student interviews (see 2 above).

8. From a recorded interview with the Head of Art, Summer Term 1987. Extracts are included throughout the chapter.

9. Written statement by student, displayed in her studio area during college post A-level student residencies, June 1987. (See *Approaching Art and Design: a guide for students* by Rod Taylor and Dot Taylor (Longman, 1990) for further plates of work and fuller account of state-ment.)

10. Student's written Personal Appraisal statement, October 1986. (Fuller account and plate in *Approaching Art and Design,* op cit.)

11. Student's written Personal Appraisal statement, October 1986. (Fuller account and plate in *Approaching Art and Design,* op cit.)

12. Student interviews (see 2 above).

13. Written statement to AEB A-level examination work, June 1988. (Addi-tional information and plate - also plates of Renu - in *Approaching Art and Design,* op cit.)

14. Interview with head teacher (op cit).

15. Student's written assignment, June 1988. (Further extract on process in *Approaching Art and Design,* op cit.)

9 Partnerships and Networks

1. Interview with head teacher, Nicol Mere (op cit).

2. From a recorded interview with Wigan's Director of Education, March 1989. This interview provides the basis for much of this chapter.

3. The reference to the 'Arts in Education' programme is to a January 1988 BBC 2 Education Programme focusing on the Wigan Education arts provision, initiatives and principles in relation to the implica-tions of the National

Curriculum as set out in the Consultation Document published during the Summer 1987.

10 Wider Developments

1. Letter from Ray Ericson to Birnie Duthie at the Department of Education, Wellington, New Zealand, following Ericson's time spent at Drumcroon and in Wigan schools during June 1987.

2. Letter from Birnie Duthie to the author, dated 23 November 1989, following a lecture tour of New Zealand by Rod Taylor as a direct consequence of Ericson's visit to Wigan.

3. Letter from Bob Birch, Perth, Australia, to the author, dated 12 November 1986, following his October 1986 visits to Drumcroon and Wigan schools.

4. Letter from Peter Hyslop, Head of Art, Diocesan College, Cape Town, to the author, January 1990, following the week long study research he spent in Wigan during May 1989.

5. Hyslop, Peter. *The Critical Studies in Art Education Project: its significance and value for South African Educators,* a report of an overseas visitorship, 1989.

6. Roger Stanley report (op cit). NB: The author has subsequently received a full report, dated 27 June 1990, of the Anne-Marie Cadman residency to which Stanley refers. It

highlights the impact the residency had on staff and pupils and how its implications are being structured into the art and design courses on offer.

7. 'An Art Critic in Residence', January 1989 Bulletin, London Borough of Barnet. (John King, the Barnet adviser, made two visits to Drumcroon during 1988, one to discuss the residency.)

8. Critical Studies Research Programme, drafted by Michele Tallack, mid 1989. Guidelines were published March 1990, and the project is now underway.

9. 'Leading the art world', *The Journal,* Leigh, 20 March 1986.

10. 'Artists in our Schools', report to the Calouste Gulbenkian Foundation on an experiment in initial teacher education, Postgraduate Art Teacher's Certificate Course, Department of Arts Education, South Glamorgan Institute of Higher Education, Autumn 1987.

11. Abbs, Peter. *Reclamations: Essays on Culture, Mass-culture and the Curriculum,* Heinemann Educational Books, 1979.

12. Evaluation by head teacher, Connaught School for Girls, Waltham Forest, of school's Autumn Term 1987 student residencies.

13. From course outline of restructuring of Polytechnic of East

London BA Honours Fine Art Course based on National Advisory Body recommendations for Fine Art Courses, Spring Term and September 1987. (Subsequent use is also made of Brunell's written evaluaton of the Polytechnic's initial phase of residencies.)

14. From a letter to the author written by Carl Sharratt, GRIST Support Teacher, Sandwell, following two visits to Drumcroon, one on 25 April 1988 and one accompanied by 12 teachers on 21 September 1989.

15. *Red Book 3: The Wigan Chapter* (op cit).

16. Vaizey, Marina. 'How 51 artists are teaching Wigan a lesson' (op cit).

Index

School Induction Pack
Adults Supporting Learning*
(Including Coaches and Volunteers)
A framework for development

association for
Physical
Education

sports coach
UK
The National Coaching Foundation

Great Coaches ... Great Sport

* Adults Supporting Learning (ASL) are those people who do not
  hold a recognised teaching qualification (although they may
  hold other relevant qualifications) but, with the permission of
  the head teacher, contribute to the delivery of physical
  education and school sport in a variety of ways.

sports coach UK is the brand name of The National Coaching Foundation and has been such since April 2001.

The British Association of Advisers and Lecturers in Physical Education (baalpe) and The Physical Education Association – United Kingdom (PEA UK) dissolved in April 2006. The Association for Physical Education (afPE) is the new physical education subject association for all professionals with appropriate qualifications in physical education, sport and dance. The regional and national networks within the Association ensure that there are opportunities for everyone involved in physical education to shape and develop the subject.

ISBN-13: 978-1-905540-28-0
ISBN-10: 1-905540-28-0

Acknowledgements

sports coach UK and afPE would like to thank the following for their involvement in the development of this pack and other supporting resources:

Emma Atkins, Paul Bickerton, Heather Moir (sports coach UK)
Sue Wilkinson, John Matthews, Eileen Marchant, Peter Whitlam (afPE)
Gill Joyce, NSPCC
Stockport Metropolitan Borough Council, Northamptonshire County Council
Birmingham City Council, Sandwell Metropolitan Borough Council
Dudley Metropolitan Borough Council, Irish Sports Council
Sports Council for Northern Ireland
Professional Development Board for Physical Education

Photographs courtesy of sports coach UK and Sport England

Throughout this publication, the pronouns he, she, him, her and so on are interchangeable and intended to be inclusive of both males and females.

sports coach UK and afPE will ensure that they have professional and ethical values and that their practices are inclusive and equitable.

© sports coach UK, 2005

Published on behalf of sports coach UK and afPE by

Coachwise Ltd
Chelsea Close
Off Amberley Road
Armley
Leeds LS12 4HP
Tel: 0113-231 1310
Fax: 0113-231 9606
Email: enquiries@coachwise.ltd.uk
Website: www.coachwise.ltd.uk

Produced and designed by **Coachwise Business Solutions**, a brand of **Coachwise** Ltd.